# God
## Unannounced

Compiled by Andy Peck
Foreword by John Arnott

# God

Bible readings and inspirational
stories from around the world

# Unannounced

CWR

Published 2011 by CWR, Waverley Abbey House, Waverley Lane, Farnham, Surrey GU9 8EP, UK. Registered Charity No. 294387. Registered Limited Company No. 1990308.

See back of book for list of National Distributors.

Concept development, editing, design and production by CWR

Printed in Finland by Bookwell.

ISBN: 978-1-85345-617-6

CONTENTS

Christians over the centuries have been fascinated by and passionate for what we now call revival. Revival is a time when God moves wonderfully in sovereign power and love. We inevitably find it unsettling, as we are not used to seeing mighty displays of the supernatural, yet we are intrigued and blessed by the awesome good fruit that remains. So it was with us in the very early months of 1994. Having prayed every morning, over a lengthy period of time, for God to come in dynamic power, we were totally surprised by the Spirit of God. We witnessed the spiritual atmosphere in our Toronto church go from comfortable and predictable, to awesome and even frightening. Yet the abundance of good fruit and the glory that was given to the Lord Jesus caused us to quickly realise that God was moving powerfully among us, the like of which we had only read about in previous revival history. To this day, people continue loving and serving the Lord Jesus with all their hearts.

There are those who do not like revival because of the apparent disorder and commotion it brings as people are powerfully touched at every level of their being: body, soul and spirit. They find the manifestations puzzling, and cannot work out how this could be God. But we have discovered time and again that it really is God, and at the end of the day it is souls saved and lives transformed and in love with Jesus that we value. We need to let God move in His own way and not quench His work when He does, and pray for more of His indescribable Presence that changes and transforms the human heart.

So what can we do to see revival come and change individuals, churches, communities and even nations? Well now, you need to read this helpful book that Andy Peck has compiled. Hear the hearts of these godly writers who are urging us to read and implement 2 Chronicles 7:14: '... if my people, who are called by my name, will humble themselves and pray and seek my face and turn from their wicked ways, then will I hear from heaven and will forgive their sin and heal their land.'

We can't make revival happen, but we can certainly position ourselves humbly before the Lord and pray and seek His face with deep repentance, and know that He desires it more than we do.

Which leaves one final question. What is in it for Him? What does the heart of Father God desire most of all from us? It has to be that we would love Him with all our heart, soul and mind (Matt. 22:37). I have been saying this for a long time. The great commandment first, and then the great commission. Hearts on fire and full of God's love are the very best witnesses to share the good news of Jesus Christ.

May revival come to you as you prayerfully read through these devotional pages. May your heart be set on fire, with the Father's love and power, and may you bear fruit that remains and brings honour and glory to our wonderful Trinitarian God.

**John Arnott**
**Catch the Fire Ministries**

When Selwyn Hughes, the founder of CWR, was looking for a name for the charity that he was forming to support churches in the UK in 1965, he settled upon Crusade for World Revival. He writes in *My Story*, his autobiography: 'I was a crusader at heart (in the sense of being a vigorous campaigner for what I believe in) and I wanted to use my voice in calling the Church to pray for and believe God for a flood of His Holy Spirit to flow through the worldwide Church.' He had observed that the fruit of the Welsh Revival had been limited by the Church's poor understanding of Scripture. He wanted to do what he could to ensure that this same mistake was not repeated. For many years he had offered his *Every Day with Jesus* Bible-reading notes free of charge providing the user promised to pray for revival in our land. Selwyn had been deeply affected by the stories of the Welsh Revival that he had heard from his parents and grandparents and longed that God would once again visit Britain in such a way. Today the ministry is known by its initials CWR, but still values those roots.

We give thanks for all the ways in which God has been manifestly at work within local churches and denominations in the UK, bringing life and vitality to churches once moribund and ineffective. But most would agree that revival has not come to these shores in the manner that Selwyn sought. Nevertheless, it remains the prayer of many that we would know such a move once again. In this book, six men who have written about or have a definite interest in revival provide us with insights from Scripture to stimulate our thinking, encourage our hearts and expand our vision for what God can do in our lives, our churches and our land.

I am grateful to Lynette Brooks, my colleague at CWR, for responding so warmly to the idea that we publish a title on the subject of revival. I am especially grateful to the six men who responded to my invitation to provide daily readings. They come from a broad theological spectrum and, to their credit, none asked who was taking part in the book before agreeing. As you read you will sense their humble passion for God and it is my prayer that their Scripture-soaked perspectives might be a means of adjusting your own particular outlook. All are authors in their own right so I would encourage you to read their work.

You will see that the weekends provide revival stories from around the world. Although there has been no widespread revival in the UK, God has been at work worldwide and I have tried to select a cross section that spans the globe. It is a mere taste of stories that are travelling around the world, and the stories selected have a wider and richer context than I have had space to cover. I have chosen stories that are in living memory – the earliest is 1982. There are many wonderful documented accounts of revivals from further back of course. I have done my best to choose accounts that are well-attested, or published elsewhere. I was looking for stories of God at work in renewal or revival that I believe most observers would say were out of the ordinary, to encourage a faith in a God who is able to work in amazing ways. We thank God for all the ways He is involved in our lives, including the apparently unremarkable. The stories are not designed to intimidate us, but create an expectation for God to move outside whatever box we may have placed Him in.

**Andy Peck 2011**

# Revival Faith

## By John Peters

## Author Profile

John Peters was born in Aberdare, South Wales, and educated at
Cardiff University and Jesus College, Oxford. He taught English
for nearly forty years, retiring in 2009. Since 1985, he has written
biographies of several significant Christian leaders, including C.S.
Lewis, Dr Martyn Lloyd-Jones, Colin Urquhart, Selwyn Hughes and,
more recently, of John and Carol Arnott. He also contributed two
chapters to the extended version of Selwyn Hughes' autobiography,
*My Story*. As a Welshman, he has always had a keen interest in the
history of revival.

John has been married to Elisabeth for almost forty-two years,
and they have three grown-up children, Daniel, Katherine and
Joanna. John is passionately interested in history and politics and
enjoys the many triumphs of Arsenal Football Club.

# Introduction

This week's verses for consideration under the overarching heading of 'Revival Faith' are 2 Chronicles 7:13–14. In *The Message* they are rendered as follows: '[If] my God-defined people, respond by humbling themselves, praying, seeking my presence, and turning their backs on their wicked lives, I'll be there ready for you: I'll listen from heaven, forgive their sins, and restore their land to health.'

This robust challenge, given against the background of the dedication of Solomon's Temple, a truly momentous event in the history of Israel, has been described by Rev Dr Selwyn Hughes, founder of CWR, in the following way: 'There is no greater passage in the whole of Scripture that shows the way to revival than 2 Chronicles 7:13–14. It is God's final and finished formula on the subject.' This forthright opinion was a familiar theme in Selwyn's writings, and in *Spoken from the Heart* (Volume 1) he dubs these verses quite unequivocally as 'God's recipe for revival', as happened in Fiji (see page 22) between 2001 and 2004.

But what did Selwyn mean by the word revival? He did not mean either renewal in general (which he saw as something confined to the Church), or a particularly impressive and powerful preaching campaign, rather he meant, in the words of Dr Martyn Lloyd-Jones, 'the Church returning to Pentecost', when God's awesome supernatural power affected the infant Church but also the world around it.

These verses may be viewed therefore as offering a most revealing insight into the whole question of 'revival and the preparation for revival', an emphasis that has been at the heart of CWR's ministry since its inception in 1965.

# A Sense of Calling

**BIBLE READING**
2 Chronicles 7:13–14

**FOCUS VERSE**
'… if my people …' (v.14)

My introduction to this week's theme suggested that revival, classically understood, has a two-fold effect: first on the Church and, second, the world. A modern historian of revival has said this: 'Revival begins when the heart of the Church is touched and [Christians] stand where the need is and relate to [ordinary] folk, and invest their lives in others.'

An important part of Christians being 'touched' is, I believe, a sense of their calling and identity as people of God. In Peter's ringing phrase, it is an awareness that they have been 'called … out of darkness into [God's] wonderful light' (1 Pet. 2:9). Paul says something similar in Ephesians chapter 1 verse 4 when he reminds his readers that God chose us '[in] Christ before the creation of the world'.

Such men and women, who have been forgiven and adopted into God's family, are also incorporated into the Church (His Body) which, in turn, has a definite role and function: to declare 'the manifold wisdom of God' to the 'rulers and authorities in the heavenly realms' (Eph. 3:10).

Viewed in this sense, it means that revival faith has its fundamental starting point in a realisation of the dignity and security we possess as children of God. What a wonderful privilege: called by God's authority and power, though of course it carries a (daily) *responsibility* with it. This should not come as a surprise to us because privilege and responsibility are twin themes in the Bible, with the preposition 'If' often playing a crucial role. Think, for example, of Matthew 6:15: 'But *if* you do not forgive men their sins, your Father will not forgive your sins'. Or John 7:37: '*If* anyone is thirsty, let him come to me and drink'. Hebrews 3:6: '… we are [God's] house, *if* we hold on to our courage and the hope of which we boast.'

It is equally true with the whole concept of revival: God will do His part, if we are sufficiently obedient to do ours. The principle to highlight here is that revival always begins with the men and women of God, those who, again in Selwyn's words, 'know Him intimately, who have taken His name upon themselves, and who are linked with Him in a family relationship'.*

**PRAYER**
**Father God, I am so grateful to be Your child. You have forgiven my sins because of Jesus' death on the cross; and I ask for the strength to live each day in a way that pleases You and gladdens Your heart. Help me to take seriously the responsibility to prepare for a future revival.**

---

*Revival: Times of Refreshing*, Selwyn Hughes (CWR, 2004).

# A True Assessment of Ourselves

**BIBLE READING**
2 Chronicles 7:13–14

**FOCUS VERSE**
'… if my people … will humble themselves …'
(v.14)

'Humility' is a scarce and undervalued commodity in today's world; and even in some Christian circles. Its root meaning, in 2 Chronicles 7:13–14, is the antithesis of pride, arrogance and self-assertion. Humble men and women accept the fact that without God's energising strength and power we are unlikely to achieve anything of lasting value and significance in God's kingdom.

It is worth remembering too that humility, in ultimate terms, is a true assessment of ourselves; and an admission that we are in desperate need of God's equipping Holy Spirit as far as revival is concerned. Why? Because revival can only be explained as the immediate (that is, mighty and direct) action and intervention of God. In this sense, God's mighty act is both sovereign (because only He can produce it) and independent of man's initiatives, however exalted and genuine they may be.

True revival, therefore, cannot be explained in purely human terms: it is a tumultuous act of the Holy Spirit, *but it can be prepared for*, as we allow the Holy Spirit to work in us. This is made explicit in Charles Haddon Spurgeon's famous 'Prayer for Revival':

> O God, send us the Holy Ghost. Give us both the breath of spiritual life and the fire of unconquerable zeal. Oh, that Thou wouldst send the wind and the fire. Thou wilt do this when we are all of one accord, all believing, all expecting, all prepared by prayer. Oh for the fire to fall again – fire which shall affect the most stolid. O God, Thou art ready to work with us, today as Thou didst then. Stay not, we beseech Thee, but work at once.

Spurgeon once preached a memorable series of sermons on the 1859 Revival, and his perceptive insight into the whole nature of revival is apparent in the prayer quoted above: when God so wishes to send the rain of revival the Holy Spirit first works in the prepared hearts of men and women; and part of that preparation includes the willingness to 'humble ourselves'. By this is meant the commitment to a particular lifestyle: holiness (Hosea said, '... seek the LORD, until he comes and showers righteousness on you', 10:12), unity (the sweeping away of denominational barriers, thus allowing the Holy Spirit free and purifying access in our lives) and prayer, which is the subject of tomorrow's comment.

**PRAYER**
**O God, help me to understand and accept that without You I am nothing. With You, I am strengthened and equipped for Your service, which includes preparing myself, in humility, for a fresh awakening of Your Holy Spirit. Break down every barrier in me and in Your Church that would inhibit the incoming of Your Spirit in power.**

# The Priority of Prayer

**BIBLE READING**
2 Chronicles 7:13–14

**FOCUS VERSE**
'... if my people ... will humble themselves and pray ...' (v.14)

As suggested in yesterday's notes, an accurate understanding of the true nature of revival commits Christians to a particular lifestyle. A fundamentally important part of that lifestyle includes prayer which one hymn-writer has characterised as 'the soul's sincere desire' and as 'the motion that burns within the breast'.

So the words of 2 Chronicles 7:13–14 are as relevant today as when they were originally written, containing a powerful progression that is both a motivator and an encouragement: 'humility ... prayer ... healing.' Humility, a true assessment of self, leads – almost inexorably – to prayer.

Charles Finney, the great revivalist, wrote: 'Sometimes the conduct of the wicked drives Christians to prayer, breaks them down and makes them tender-hearted, so that they can weep night and day and instead of scolding the wicked, they pray earnestly for them. Then they may expect revival.' Finney's words are endorsed by the well-known Bible commentator, Matthew Henry, who said: 'When God is about to do a great work in the world first He sets His people a-praying.'

Dedicated and consistent prayer of this sort is frequently linked by revival historians with fasting as a necessary prelude to a spiritual awakening. This emphasis on *prayer and fasting* was a key feature of the eighteenth-century revival under the leadership of the Wesley brothers and George Whitefield. In fact, John Wesley was so convinced of this power that he urged early Methodists to fast every Wednesday and Friday. Typically, he felt so strongly about the necessity for fasting on these two days that he refused to ordain anyone as a Methodist minister unless they complied with his wishes in this respect. Such a strategy is not being advocated in these notes, but it is salutary to remember that such men as Luther, Calvin, Andrew Murray and Lloyd-Jones were all convinced of the need for prayer *and* fasting.

Permit me, too, at this point to remind readers of some delightfully personal words by Selwyn Hughes:

> There is a date in the history of revivals that I love very much. It is April 20th 1928 – seven days before I was born. A group of people were praying for revival to come to [my home] village when they were led by the Holy Spirit to combine their prayer time with several days of fasting. Within a few weeks the Holy Spirit came to the village in awesome power. Some of the hardest of miners were converted and a church was formed in which many years later I myself found Christ.

**PRAYER**
**Heavenly Father, I so thank You for the resource and encouragement of prayer, but regret that so often I am prayer-less. Please forgive me, and remind me daily through Your Holy Spirit that prayer, far from being a duty, is a delight. Help me also to realise that fasting releases the Holy Spirit to do His special work of revival in Your people.**

# Prayer Leading to Repentance

**BIBLE READING**
2 Chronicles 7:13–14

**FOCUS VERSE**
'... pray and seek my face and turn from their wicked ways ...' (v.14)

Most Christians, in theory at least, subscribe to the view that there's nothing more powerful than prayer, especially when it is the 'sincere desire that burns within the breast'.

Duncan Campbell, the human face of the last major revival in Britain (The Hebridean Revival, 1949–52), has recorded an occasion when he simply could not get on with preaching the message God had laid on his heart. So he stopped preaching and asked a young man, James Cameron, to pray. Rather startlingly, the boy stood up and asked. 'What is the use in praying if we are not right with God?' This pertinent question was followed by a reading from Psalm 24, including verses 3–4: 'Who may ascend the hill of the LORD? ... He who has clean hands and a pure heart ...'. In fact, the young boy, after reciting the whole of the psalm, began to pray.

Suddenly after about twenty minutes he said, 'Excuse me, Lord, while I resist the devil.' With that, he turned around and commanded the devil to leave. A further 45 minutes of prayer followed, and when he finished praying it was as if God had turned on a switch in heaven, and the Spirit of God fell on that church, that community, and revival was born.

From a slightly different perspective, revival historians also suggest that *prayer accompanied by repentance* is a necessary prerequisite to Holy Spirit inspired revival. When Martin Luther nailed his 95 Theses to the church door at Wittenburg one of his first statements read: 'When our Lord Jesus Christ said "repent", he meant the entire life of the believer should be one of repentance.' Much the same was said by William Booth, the founder of the Salvation Army, at the start of the twentieth-century when he spoke about 'a religion without the Holy Spirit, Christianity without Christ, and *forgiveness without repentance*' (my italics).

But what do we need to repent of today? Each of us would have our own list, but may I suggest the following: denominationalism, lukewarmness and a lack of spiritual passion, a tendency to compromise when our Christian conscience is bombarded by the attacks of a world in which Satan reigns, and a resistance to the pleadings of the Holy Spirit to repent. Steve Hill, who had an important role in the Pensacola Revival (1995 onwards), puts it dramatically: 'A Time to Weep.' Spiritual revival begins when we put God first and desire Him above everything and everyone else.

**PRAYER**
**Lord Jesus, I come to You now with all my weakness and all my emptiness. I give my life into Your hands, now fill me with Your Spirit so that every part of me shall be Yours, indwelt by You, dominated by You. I give you all the glory and all the honour. Lord Jesus, send revival, I pray, and start with me.**

# The Heart of Revival

**BIBLE READING**
2 Chronicles 7:13–14

**FOCUS VERSE**
'... then will I hear from heaven and will forgive ... and will heal their land.' (v.14)

A pertinent question brings to a conclusion this week's notes: what is the true nature of revival? Or indeed: what is the heart of true revival?

May I suggest that it is to be found in:

1 **The sovereignty of God.** Not even the most gifted of preachers can manufacture revival, it is heaven-sent. Only God can bring it into being, although unwise decisions can bring it to an end, as revival history all too sadly demonstrates. While God's sovereignty is absolutely central to any consideration of revival, it is also true that it can be **prepared for** as this week's key verses show. So what is the link between a sovereign God and men and women longing for another Holy Spirit inspired awakening? Some words by Brian Mills, in *Preparing for Revival*, provide the answer: 'Prayer is the means whereby the longing of man and the will of God become one.'

2 **The presence of God.** God is so powerfully operative in revival that such 'times of refreshing'

seem like days of heaven on earth; and nothing else matters when compared with the thrill of intimacy with our all-loving heavenly Father. Immersion in the glory of God is an unforgettable experience.

3 **The love of God**. God's glory and God's love are inextricably linked in revival. It is the sort of love that flows – without stop or hindrance – between the Persons of the Trinity and from them outwards towards the world and, in particular, the people of God.

4 **Ruthless dealing with sin**. Lives that please God must not tolerate sin, however attractive it may appear outwardly. This was something Evan Roberts highlighted both before and during the Welsh Revival 1904–05, and it was an emphasis I noticed when visiting the Pensacola Revival, Florida, in the year 2000. One Sunday morning I attended the Children's Church, consisting of 400 children between the ages of six and twelve. They prayed, interceded, worshipped and listened to three sessions of serious teaching on 'losing your first love' which included comments on 'how to deal with sin in our lives'.

5 **Exalting Jesus**. In revival, Jesus is restored to His position as the Supreme Head of the Church. The Apostle Peter, in his sermon before the Sanhedrin (Acts 4), aptly characterises Jesus as the 'only' source of salvation; and in revival this grips the hearts and minds of men and women, not as mere theory but as a motive for living. Surely our reaction to an appreciation of the true nature of revival is: 'Lord, do it again'.

**PRAYER**
**O God, I pray that You will give me a burning passion for You that reflects Your burning love for Your people – for me. Dear Lord, baptise me afresh with heavenly fire. Give me a Pentecost. Scatter Your refining fire through every part of my life so that my heart is ready and open for You to move in and through me whatever the cost. Lord, send the fire.**

# Fiji –
# The Healing
# of the Land

The movement of God on the islands of Fiji touched those at the heart of the government of the nation and also those with barely enough to eat.

Fiji, a former British Colony, comprises 322 islands in the South Pacific Ocean, 18 degrees south of the Equator and 1,100 miles north of New Zealand. There are two main islands and just over 100 other inhabited islands. It became independent in the 1970s and has 54% of the population native Fiji and 28% of a Polynesian/Indian background.

Two military coups in 1987 were followed by another in 2000, in which all the members of parliament were held hostage for fifty-six days. This led to looting, vandalism, rioting and violence on the streets. Many business premises were destroyed. The economy collapsed, there was mutiny in the army and the outlook seemed very bleak.

Soul-searching took place among the leaders who felt that disunity among the churches was linked to the divisions in society. The president called the church leaders together and called them to unite. Previously, many churches and denominations had sought renewal and revival, but separately.

Now they realised they had to come together, for the answer to Fiji's situation could come from God alone. So they called the members of all the churches to accept their responsibility for the state of the nation and to pray for God to change the situation.

In July 2001, Christians joined together for three weeks of prayer and Bible teaching choosing 2 Chronicles 7:14 as their motto. The Association of Christian Churches in Fiji (ACCF) was officially founded with four aims: i) to unite all churches; ii) to put God's way of love into practice; iii) to establish God-fearing leaders; iv) to see reconciliation in Fiji, to create peace and prosperity.

At the end of the three weeks, a crowd of 10,000 people gathered to hear the acting prime minister speak to them. As a general election was about to take place, they expected his speech to make political points, but instead he spoke of the need to put the nation right in the eyes of God:

> Our efforts in building this country will come to nothing, if they are not rooted firmly in the love and fear of God. I ask Him to forgive me for the times I have been neglectful and cold in my relationship with Him. With Your guidance, Lord, this sinner will renew himself; will find new purpose in the pursuit of Your will. Lord, I entreat You, again, to forgive me, to save me, to capture my heart and hold my hand. I honor You as the King of Kings.[1]

The prayer for reconciliation and the move of God in the islands of Fiji included specific prayer that the very land might be healed as 2 Chronicles 7:14 promises: '... if my people, who are called by my name, will humble themselves and pray and seek my face and turn from their wicked ways, then will I hear from heaven and will forgive their sin and will *heal their land*' (emphasis added).

'Healing the Land' teams were formed, made up of people who dedicated themselves to a full year of prayer and fasting for their nation (typically this was 6am to 3pm daily). The ministry's leader, Pastor Vuniani, had been seeking the Lord for his nation for twenty years, together with a number of pastors from the wider Pacific region. For him fasting for his nation had become a lifestyle. The Healing the Land team was thus ready to travel to regions and villages when the desperation there about the local situation became so urgent that the whole village, led by churches in that area that wanted to work with them, agreed to pray and fast with repentance.

They would be sent into villages or respond to invitations, and lead the village elders, pastors and fathers through teaching and prayer in further confession of sins and conversion, in restoration of relationships with other villages and tribes, among the tribe itself, and with the regional and national government.

Stories of the way God answered prayer abound. In the coastal village of Nataleira there was division, tension and strife. Idolatry and witchcraft created an atmosphere of evil, with many people dying untimely deaths. Even among the Christians there was prejudice, rivalry and division. Young people were taking drugs and sleeping around. There seemed to be a general spirit of rebellion against parents and all authority. The soil produced very few crops, and when the villagers went to the forest to try and grow crops, these were rooted up and destroyed by wild animals, especially pigs. At sea, the coral reef had died, so there were no fish to be caught.

In 2004, things were brought to a head when the locals had been stirred up by the death of a young man – a suicide which seemed to be connected to his inadvertent disturbing of an idol when he was out riding. Suicide was unheard of within the village, and a shocked community gathered with the village elders to discuss what should be done.

At the meeting they decided to call in the Healing the Land team. The team went to the village, found out the facts, and told the people they had to fast and pray for two weeks, which they did.

Two weeks later, the team arrived back, and while they were there they did a prayer walk round the village every evening for seven nights. On the seventh night, they blew on shells, banged on cymbals and commanded the demons to leave the village. The demons left, and it was reported that all the dogs in the village barked as they did so.

During their time there, the team prophesied that fire would fall in the village. As the mission went on, people repented of their sins, of their prejudice and division. The young people repented of their rebelliousness and their disobedience to their parents. People wept and cried as they were reconciled to each other.

On the last night of the mission, the villagers brought all their witchcraft items and put them in a pile to be burnt. Then a man named Amosi, spoke up and said, 'It isn't right for these idols to stay here. They must be destroyed.' So the young people went out and broke them up, and put the pieces on top of the bonfire.

On the following day, after the team had left, and as it was getting dark, the mother of the boy who had committed suicide was standing with some others when she saw an intense light over the sea. It was a wide column of fire, rising high over the surface, glowing red, orange and yellow, with flames at the side, which spread out over a large area of the sea. This magnificent sight stayed in position for about half an hour, and was a fulfilment of the prophecy that fire would come to the village. The very next day, when they went out to fish, there was a huge shoal of fish. It would seem that God had healed the coral reef and brought the fish back. Everybody came and caught an abundance of fish, filling large 50-kilogram bags again and again. And on the land, the crops started to grow again.

Since then, the villagers come together for prayer meetings every Wednesday, from 6am to 3pm, to coincide with the times of fasting. On the first Sunday of every month they unite in worship together, and every six months they have a week of united meetings. The locals have put up a monument there to commemorate the happenings in 2004, erected on the site where the witchcraft items were burnt. On the monument they have put the dates of the transformation: 16 May 2004 to 14 June 2004, and the proclamation that there is no God but Jehovah, quoting Isaiah 43:11, and that He is the God of Nataleira.

Reports from around the nation in villages are abundant: it is believed that the gospel has been preached in over 200 villages within the islands of Fiji. Couples who have been barren for ten to twenty years are now having children (some parents at fifty years of age); once low-yield fruit trees are now producing fruit twelve months of the year; fish that have been absent for fifty years are plentiful. In addition to the ecological wonders, entire villages have committed their hearts to Jesus, the national government is working alongside a unified Church and reconciliation is taking place on many levels. This is revival leading to transformation.

The economy also began to recover – the number of jobs is growing, and unemployment decreasing. The building industry is booming, with ever more complex projects. The hotels are fully booked, and there is not enough accommodation to meet the demand.

Surely God has fulfilled His promise in 2 Chronicles 7:14!

---

1. Information from the Sentinel Group 2005 video/DVD, *Let the Sea Resound* (www.glowtorch.org).

1. What words come into your mind when you think about humility? Does humility link with a healthy self-esteem?

2. In what ways could your church be said to be 'ready for revival'? In what ways is it not?

3. Charles Finney exhorts us to pray rather than 'scold'. Are there individuals or types of people you want to scold rather than pray for?

4. What do you truly long for? Does God have anything to do with your longings?

**5**. Brian Mills says: 'Prayer is the means whereby the longing of man and the will of God become one.' Is this true of your prayer times?

**6**. The word repentance comes from a root word which means 'change of mind'. Thinking of your walk with God, what have you had to change your mind about recently?

**7**. Are you surprised that God has a concern for the land in Fiji, as well as the people? See Romans 8:18–22.

**8**. Does God, in your view, have a particular concern for Britain?

# Preparing for Transforming Revival

By George Otis Jr

## Author Profile

George Otis Jr serves as president of The Sentinel Group, a Seattle-based research, media, and training organisation that produces the widely-acclaimed *Transformations* documentary series. Since the late 1990s, Mr Otis and his team have investigated hundreds of transformed communities throughout the world. More recently, their observations have been distilled into a comprehensive training process, called The Journey to Transformation, that is designed to help revival-hungry communities prepare for Divine visitation. Mr Otis is currently working to extend these and other revival-related resources via the ministry's interactive website (www.glowtorch.org), and an emerging network of service partners.

# Introduction

While the Scriptures are brimming with wonderful and insightful passages on revival, it took some searching to come up with a single text capable of supporting a week's worth of meaty lessons. When I came across Isaiah 57:5–58:12, however, I knew I had tapped into a rich vein of revival principles. In this passage, which spans portions of two chapters, we find lessons on 'good hopelessness', 'preparation and humility', 'compromised fasting', 'summoning divine presence' and 'reclaiming a corporate identity'. While, at first glance, these topics seem to have little in common, a deeper investigation reveals them to be essential and interrelated threads in the tapestry of transforming revival.

For many Christians, the subject of revival is abstract and mysterious. In some quarters, misguided notions of divine sovereignty have led believers to conclude there is nothing they can do to prepare for an awakening or visitation. As my good friend Peter Horrobin puts it, many people tend to view revivals as if they were pizza pies that God fashions on the moon and occasionally flings to earth. There they land, seemingly without warning, on the left shoulders of unsuspecting passers-by. This notion may be widespread, but as we shall see, it is hardly biblical.

I have chosen to put the whole Bible text each day rather than pick out just one verse.

# The Benefits of Hopelessness

**BIBLE READING**
Isaiah 57:5–10

> You burn with lust among the oaks
>   and under every spreading tree;
> you sacrifice your children in the ravines
>   and under the overhanging crags.
> The idols among the smooth stones of the
>     ravines are your portion;
>   they, they are your lot ...
> Behind your doors and your doorposts
>   you have put your pagan symbols.
> Forsaking me, you uncovered your bed,
>   you climbed into it and opened it wide ...
>   you descended to the grave itself!
> You were wearied by all your ways,
>   but you would not say, 'It is hopeless.'
> You found renewal of your strength,
>   and so you did not faint.

The underlying assumption behind words like revival, awakening, reformation (or whatever your favourite term for societal change happens to be), is that a dysfunctional status quo has been, or needs to be, made new by the power and presence of the living God. In the passage above, the prophet Isaiah describes a society in need of just such a touch. A society, not unlike our own, that is in steep decline.

It's all there. Lust. Violence. Idolatry. Family breakdown. False covenants. All pursued with a vigour that is characteristic of a society in moral heat. But the high is difficult to sustain. In time, amidst all the searching, groping and uncovering, relationships become twisted. Pleasure turns to pain. The accumulated weight of sin becomes burdensome. Suddenly there are no good times any more. '*You descended to the grave itself!*' Isaiah exclaims. '*You were wearied by all your ways.*'

The condition is painful, but it comes with a flash of hope. When individuals and societies are shorn of their strength and awash in desperation, the conditions are ripe for deliverance. Struggle gives way to submission. Corners become doorways. But then, on the very cusp of surrender, disaster strikes! Instead of giving up and allowing God to rescue them, the community finds a second wind. '... *you would not say, "It is hopeless". You found renewal of your strength ...*' This last-second grasping is most readily seen in self-sufficient Western cultures. We go to bed convinced the end has come, but then wake up the following morning with a fresh idea. Reaching deep into our bag of reserves, we pull out one last programme. And so revival tarries.

**PRAYER**
**God, show us the folly of self-deliverance. Bring us to the end of ourselves so that YOU can begin to work Your magic.**

# Preparation and Humility

## BIBLE READING
Isaiah 57:14–15

'Build up, build up, prepare the road!
   Remove the obstacles out of the way
      of my people.'
For this is what the high and lofty
   One says –
   he who lives for ever, whose name is holy:
"I live in a high and holy place,
   but also with him who is contrite and
      lowly in spirit,
to revive the spirit of the lowly
   and to revive the heart of the contrite."'

Whatever else may be said about transforming revival, most Christians will agree that it cannot take place apart from the presence of God. The challenge, then, is to discover why His presence is missing, and what steps are essential to its restoration.

In verse 14, Isaiah admonishes us to 'prepare the road'. And the business of preparing for revival is quite distinct from any attempt to *plan* for it. Though the latter is much in vogue in the formulaic West – with some going so far as to announce calendar dates for the Spirit's appearance – it is simply not possible to stage-manage the appearance of a King! This does not mean that we are relegated to idleness or monastic contemplation in the seasons that precede revival. The Scriptures clearly instruct us to make ready for God's presence (see Isa. 40:3; Mal. 3:1; and Luke 1:17). As the Father articulates through Isaiah, this involves 'removing obstacles' that block the road to reconciliation. No obstacle is more deterring to revival than human pride. Not only does God abhor it (Prov. 6:16–17; Amos 6:8), but He actively resists anyone foolish enough to wear its cloak (Jer. 50:31; James 4:6).

According to Psalm 138:6, He knows the proud, but only 'from afar'. Conversely, God will draw up close to the humble. In verse 15 of our text, we learn that the Almighty lives 'in a high and holy place, but *also* with him who is contrite and lowly in spirit ...' The implications of this duality of divine presence are remarkable. If the 'high and lofty place' is where God's governance requires Him to be, the company of the humble is where He *chooses* to dwell. In this sense, the lowly and contrite represent His 'country cottage', the place where He retreats for enjoyment.

**PRAYER**
**Heavenly Father, help us to prepare a place for You to tabernacle among us, and may the humility of our hearts bring You deep and sustained satisfaction.**

# Compromised Fasting

## ISAIAH 58:2–4

'For day after day they seek me out;
   they seem eager to know my ways,
as if they were a nation that does what is right
   and has not forsaken the commands of its God.
They ask me for just decisions
   and seem eager for God to come near them.
"Why have we fasted," they say,
   "and you have not seen it?
Why have we humbled ourselves,
   and you have not noticed?"
'Yet on the day of your fasting, you do
      as you please
   and exploit all your workers.
Your fasting ends in quarrelling and strife,
   and in striking each other with wicked fists.
You cannot fast as you do today
   and expect your voice to be heard on high.'

This well-known passage offers up a stark reminder that it is eminently possible for God's people to operate according to a set of religious assumptions that He does not share. In this case, the fault rests in the notion that we can establish separate standards for relating to God and our fellow man. We may try to, but He will have none of it. Even though the Israelites sought God on a daily basis and seemed 'eager to know [His] ways', their divided hearts and inconsistent behaviour caused Him to tune them out. Yet, for some inexplicable reason, they apparently assumed that He either didn't care about their misdeeds, or that their religious devotion caused Him to look the other way. 'Why have we fasted ... and you have not seen it?' they asked. 'Why have we humbled ourselves, and you have not noticed?' They seemed genuinely baffled. If we are serious about summoning God's presence and attention, we must remember that He is a heart reader, not a lip reader. When we treat others badly, it is as if we are directing our behaviour towards God Himself. No amount of church attendance, fasting or Bible reading will mitigate our culpability. If we love our sin enough to harbour it, then God will simply ignore our prayers (Psa. 66:18).

Our journey to transforming revival must begin with utter transparency. There can be no religious exemptions. No carefully crafted explanations. In the end, it is His assessment that counts. Not ours.

**PRAYER**
**Oh God, show us our hearts as You see them. Shine Your light on any concealed bitterness or uncleanness. And as we confess our sin before You, cleanse us and receive our prayers.**

# Summoning His Presence

## ISAIAH 58:6–9

'Is not this the kind of fasting I have chosen:
to loose the chains of injustice
   and untie the cords of the yoke,
to set the oppressed free
   and break every yoke?
Is it not to share your food with the hungry
   and to provide the poor wanderer with shelter –
when you see the naked, to clothe him,
   and not to turn away from your own flesh
     and blood?
Then your light will break forth like
   the dawn,
   and your healing will quickly appear;
then your righteousness will go before you,
   and the glory of the LORD will be your rear guard.
Then you will call, and the LORD will answer;
   you will cry for help, and he will say: Here am I.'

If God is resistant to religious hypocrisy, He has all the time in the world for men and women whose hearts mirror His values. Although King David was a flawed individual, his transparency, fairness and headlong pursuit after righteousness, made him 'a man after [God's] own heart' (Acts 13:22).

So, strange as it may seem to religious traditionalists, efforts to reach out to the hungry and oppressed have the same summoning power as a committed fast. Many people just assume that revival is ushered in by long fasts and stadiums filled with praying people. But God's attention is not secured by religious devotion, or by numbers. His question is not, 'How many people are praying?' but rather, '*Who* is praying?' This is important to remember when we get discouraged that others are not exhibiting the same level of appetite for revival that we have.

While it is true that revival is a consequence of unity, this accord is often between a relatively small group of people. Unity is not unanimity, and those who hold out for the latter may be in for a long wait. And, again, revival is not the product of unity alone. Other factors, such as humility, hunger and even compassion, also draw the presence of God. At the end of the day, it is simply a matter of embracing the values of His heart. As we do this, Isaiah says, *then* He will answer our prayers. We will call for help, and He will say: '*Here am I.*'

**PRAYER**
**Lord, teach us Your ways that we might embrace them as our own. We desperately want – and need – You to draw near to us.**

# Reclaiming a Corporate Identity

## ISAIAH 58:11–12

'The LORD will guide you always;
    he will satisfy your needs in a sun-scorched land
    and will strengthen your frame.
You will be like a well-watered garden,
    like a spring whose waters never fail.
Your people will rebuild the ancient ruins
    and will raise up the age-old foundations;
you will be called Repairer of Broken Walls,
    Restorer of Streets with Dwellings.'

This passage speaks of what can happen when we exchange the yoke of oppression and malicious talk for a heart of humility and service to others. The benefits are almost too glorious to contemplate. Darkness swept away, perpetual divine guidance, a meeting of physical and emotional needs, and fruitfulness without end. Anyone searching for a description of personal transformation need look no further. Isaiah, however, mentions one final characteristic of a revived people that warrants our attention. Often overlooked, it speaks to an issue that lies at the very heart of transforming revival: *identity*.

This identity is initially seen at a personal level. Revived people are made whole, but not simply to enjoy themselves. Rather, they are strengthened and prospered by God in order that they might serve as *societal change agents.* Isaiah starts by telling us what these change agents *do* ('rebuilding ancient ruins'), and then describes what they are *called* ('Repairers of Broken Walls' and 'Restorers of Streets with Dwellings'). Revived people, in other words, have a reputation for improving things.

But while the presence of God restores personal identity, it does precisely the same thing for communities. Apart from God, cities and towns are merely collections of spiritually homeless people – people who don't know who they are or where they are going. To find some sense of corporate identity, unredeemed communities often look to landmarks, festivals, corporate headquarters or sports franchises. In the end, however, none of these sources will suffice.

Conversely, when God is welcomed into a community, His very presence galvanizes purpose and identity (see Isa. 1:26; 62:12; Ezek. 48:35). In Guatemala, for instance, the transformed community of Almolonga is often referred to as 'The City of God'. Similarly, in the United States, the City Council of Manchester, Kentucky, recently renamed their revived community, 'The City of Hope'.

**PRAYER**
**Thank You, Father, for the marvellous power of Your redemptive presence in our lives and communities. Revive us that we might go forth as Your change agents into a world in need of identity.**

# Wales – House of Prayer

**R**oy Godwin, fifty-five, feared he was in a spiritual backwater. An evangelist and pastor, who had known and experienced God's touch during the Charismatic Renewal in the late seventies and early eighties, he now found himself running a Christian retreat centre, Ffald-y-Brenin (Sheepfold of the King, pronounced *fald er breneen*) with his wife, Daphne, in the hills by the sea in North Pembrokeshire, southwest Wales. His desire to serve God had begun in his mid teens, spurred by a book, *The Revival We Need* by Oswald J. Smith on the Welsh Revivals of 1904, and a longing to see God breathe upon people, change their hearts and use them.

Roy had previously enjoyed a fruitful ministry within the business community, and yearned for contact with the 'real world', where he could see people coming to faith once again, but recent years had been hard and a business venture had collapsed. Indeed, the first words of the book which outlines what God did at Ffald-y-Brenin, *The Grace Outpouring*,[1] are the words of Roy, 'I was desperate'.

Initially, Roy had been reluctant to accept the position of Centre Director at Ffald-y-Brenin, having decided against it when he saw what the job entailed. Instead, he accepted a lucrative commercial consultancy position. During the training week, he became increasingly uncomfortable, and realised that God was not in it. However, he had spent some money given in advance by the firm and was in no position to repay it. After internal wrestling he concluded that he'd rather have God than money, and when he explained the situation to the MD he was staggered to discover that not only was he happy to allow him to leave, he could keep the money too. That very evening a phone call came from the trustees of Ffald-y-Brenin, saying that despite a completed interview process with recruits for the post the trustees felt Roy was the man for the job even though Roy was still not willing to consider it!

But Roy was still uncertain, and it took a series of remarkable events to convince him that he was in just the right place.

Roy and Daphne had begun work at the centre when, out of the blue, a couple knocked at the door, declaring that they had been strangely led to the place and wanted to know more. Roy showed them around and, before they left, decided to pray a blessing over them. A moment of intense encounter with the Holy Spirit took place, and prayer over visitors became a new pattern.

In the following days a steady flow of people turned up at the centre, uninvited, strangely drawn by an inexplicable inner prompting.

On one occasion a couple arrived, the husband confused about the way he had been compelled to steer his car up the drive. Roy recalls his discomfort when the husband told a decidedly blue joke in their kitchen. But God reassured Roy that He was involved. Roy and Daphne showed the couple around, with the husband still sharing profane stories. They arrived at the chapel and were ushered in, whereupon the husband fell down and experienced a profound sense of

God's presence. Crying out to Him he said: 'I'm so sorry. I didn't know You were real. I've heard so much about You and not really believed, and not cared, but I didn't know You were real. Oh God, I'm so dirty. Oh God, how can You ever cleanse me? Oh God, can You ever have mercy on me?'[2] His wife's legs gave way too, and she also sat and wept.

Roy and Daphne left God to do His work.

Roy relates some of the extraordinary events that took place at the centre:

- As a leader prays for a few minutes before breakfast an angel appears in the room and the voice of God is heard. She calls her team together and an amazing depth of healing and cleansing takes place. This continues until Midnight.
- Bonfires are lit before the High Cross [a wooden cross they felt led to erect] in the grounds as people physically surrender things to Jesus. Dustbin bags have to be used to remove the excess rubbish.
- Children agree to come on a Church Weekend as long as it's a secret and their friends don't find out. Suddenly they are filled with the Holy Spirit and speak in new tongues as Jesus appears to them. They go to school and ask the Head for permission to start a school prayer meeting, and start to witness enthusiastically to their friends.
- A carload of guests, swapping jokes as they approach our drive, suddenly have to pull off the road because the Holy Spirit falls on them ...
- Two atheists in their 20s (visiting with Christian friends) discover they are lost as the God they don't believe in reveals Himself to them. As they respond they are filled with the Spirit and the joy of the Lord floods their hearts; they shout praises until the early hours.

• A Church leaders' weekend retreat – Saturday is listed as a
free day, but they pray before breakfast. The glory of God
appears and they don't get their breakfast – or their lunch, or
their tea. So they decide that the next day will be their free
day. But the same thing happens again.[3]

The move of God in the centre paralleled a move God was
doing in Roy. Roy sensed that God wanted the centre to be
a 'House of Prayer' and that He would show him the unique
way in which this would become a reality in rural Wales. God
showed Roy that before the centre would become a House of
Prayer – Roy himself would become a House of Prayer.

People are not just touched through prayer; people who
walk near the boundary of the garden surrounding the guest
house become aware of a 'presence'. This included a couple
knocked off their feet by a power they had never experienced
before but which seemed to answer a longing they had had
all their lives.

Roy Godwin and Dave Roberts describe one couple's
story related to guests at the centre: 'When we walk on the
path near the boundary, it's as though we're drunk and our
legs won't hold us up, and we feel full of inexpressible joy.
And we've found that if we get closer to the boundary it's
stronger, but if we manage to crawl away it sort of lifts. Can
you explain what's going on?'[4]

The couple met with Roy and Daphne and started a journey
towards faith in Christ.

Tradespeople are also aware of the presence. One left the
premises before his work was completed because it made him
so uncomfortable; another lingered, not wanting to leave.

There have been seasons when healings were especially
common. A 32-year-old woman, who had had chronic

osteoarthritis since her early 20s which confined her to a wheelchair, came to the centre just before an operation. Roy prayed for her, with no apparent result. It was only when she was talking with the specialist prior to her operation that she sensed God's healing touch and said that she didn't believe she needed surgery, whereupon she got out of the wheelchair, walked around the office and was eventually discharged by the startled doctor.

Many receive inner healing, with guests testifying to God waking them in the night and speaking tenderly to them of the way He would heal the wounds that afflicted them.

But the place is not always a place of high excitement. The work of the Spirit there ebbs and flows. Sometimes God does a much deeper work in people visiting during 'ebb' times than when the Spirit is in full 'flow'.

Roy and his team long for similar Houses of Prayer to be established across the world. Roy believes that at the heart of any House of Prayer should be a willingness to be a blessing and to speak blessing into the local community.

He has what he calls 'three Caleb Key Questions', which he encourages those who want to form Houses of Prayer to ask of themselves. They can be summarised in this way:

1. What is good and wholesome within this community that we could bless?
2. Who is God putting in front of us to whom we might show mercy or kindness?
3. Who is God putting in front of us with whom we might share the gospel? (See *The Grace Outpouring*, page 163.)

A section of Roy's website aims to provide a supportive online community for those wishing to set up their own Houses of Prayer.[5]

On the website are these words:

> We invite others to join in our commitment to pray these words every day, as we do at Ffald-y-Brenin:

> O High King of heaven,
> Have mercy on our Land.
> Revive your Church;
> Send the Holy Spirit for the sake of the children.
> May your kingdom come to our nation.
> In Jesus' mighty name.
> Amen.[6]

---

**Notes**

1. Ray Godwin and Dave Roberts, *The Grace Outpouring: Blessing others through prayer* (Eastbourne: David C. Cook, Kingsway, 2008).
2. Ibid., p.21.
3. www.anglicanrenewalministries-wales.org.uk/main/magazine/issue33/RGodwin.htm
4. *The Grace Outpouring*, op. cit., p.89.
5. www.ffald-y-brenin.org/caleb-community
6. www.ffald-y-brenin.org/ministries/the-caleb-prayer

1 Have you ever been at 'the end of yourself'? Did this become an opportunity for God to work, or did you simply have a new idea that got you going again?

2. Many of us depend upon qualifications for our role in life, whether this be university, apprenticeship, or the hard graft of experience. Do these things make us too proud to depend on God?

3. Is there anyone you know who is 'humble and contrite'?

4. 'If we love our sin enough to harbour it, then God will simply ignore our prayers (Psa. 66:18).' Do you assume God always hears you? How might this change the way you pray?

5. 'It's not how many pray but who prays.' Do you know anyone with a particular prayer ministry? What can you learn from such people?

6. Does the presence of your church in the community have any effect? How might you pray that it would?

7. Have you ever sensed the 'manifest presence' of God so powerfully that it was tangible? How might you know it was God?

8. Look again at the three Caleb questions. How would you respond to them within your situation?

# Praying With Your Eyes Open
### By Greg Haslam

## Author Profile

Greg Haslam was born and raised in Liverpool. He is married to Ruth and they have three grown-up sons and two granddaughters. He studied Theology and History at Durham University. After teaching in high school he trained for the ministry at the London Theological Seminary before moving to Winchester where he pastored for 21 years until his call to Westminster Chapel, London in March 2002.

Greg has travelled widely as a preacher and conference speaker, both in the UK and overseas. He believes strongly in the recovery of strong healthy churches, characterised by a strong and vigorous God-centred focus. This is manifested primarily in a renewed confidence in God's Word, and a conscious engagement with His Spirit. Such churches bring hope to the world!

He is the author of many articles and six books. The latest include *Preach the Word!* (Sovereign World), *A Radical Encounter with God* (New Wine Press), *Moving in the Prophetic* (Monarch Books) and *The Man Who Wrestled With God* (New Wine Press). He has also contributed to the recently published *Should Christians Embrace Evolution?* (IVP).

# Introduction

The figure of righteous Daniel towers over the violent upheavals of invasion and exile experienced by the nation of Israel during the ruthless totalitarian regimes of Babylon and Persia, under Nebuchadnezzar and Darius.

Immediately juxtaposed with Daniel's revival prayer is his earlier vision of future horrors that left him feeling violently sick (Dan. 8:27)! Nausea and fraught emotions are appropriate for God's people today. The Church in the West is in 'exile' too – a condition we've often experienced under the chastening hand of God – the result of unfaithfulness, idolatry, rebellion, failure to preach the gospel, and seek the Holy Spirit's power. '*Whom the Lord loves he beats the hell out of*' (Heb. 12:6, my paraphrase).

Hence, 'Exile' – the tragedy of loss and displacement in a foreign land, a 'Babylonian Captivity' of changed landscapes where the Church adopts the methods of big business, and the methods of show business, performing like spiritual 'snake oil' salesmen to win a crowd. Past glories fade. Future hope seems impossible. Homesick and nostalgic, we see ourselves as a weak and irrelevant minority in a strange new world of religious pluralism that holds all the best advertising space. Our beliefs seem 'outdated' in a climate that denies that Truth exists at all, defining God as a figment of fevered religious imaginations and an insult to human dignity.

It's hard to sing the Lord's songs in a foreign land (Psa. 137:4). But prayer for revival may yet move God to bring us all back home.

# 'Spirit and Word-Ignited Prayer'

**BIBLE READING**
Daniel 9:1–3

**FOCUS VERSE**
'... I, Daniel, understood from the Scriptures ...'
(v.2)

In 539 BC, 11 yrs after Daniel's emotional illness in 8:27, Babylon had fallen to Persian rule under King Darius. Daniel was over 80 years old, and overwhelmed again. History is a mystery. Prophetic people are the Church's eyes and ears. They ask, '*Why do shattering events happen?*', then look and listen for God to speak to them. Ignorance is not bliss. Prophets are rarely content not to know, if knowing is possible. Matthew Henry said that when God intends to do something great for His people He usually 'sets them to praying'. Secular-minded Christians struggle to believe God changes history. Bible people don't. Movements of men and nations are but the scaffolding God erects to build His Church and everlasting kingdom. So, God re-awakens His 'sleeper agents' to take action.

Daniel's distress led to a resolve to fast and pray. Two things followed: (1) *He devoured the*

*Scriptures* (v.2a). Daniel received extraordinary revelations, hearing directly from God. But he read the Bible too – Jeremiah, not our favourite book. Daniel pored over and scaled Bible peaks we find hard to climb. Don't divorce the Spirit from Word – '*What God has joined together let no man put asunder*'. The Word awakens thirst for the Spirit; the Spirit stirs hunger for the Word. No wonder Daniel treasured Jeremiah as self-attesting scripture, eagerly devouring what we might have neglected. We can't 'dump' any Bible book. How important is the whole Bible to you?

(2) *He was invigorated by the Scriptures* (v.3). Lutheran Pastor Martin Niemoller suffered under the Nazis. His guards confiscated everything, including his Bible. He recalled, 'This first night I shall never forget, because I didn't sleep for one minute. I didn't find any peace. I was quarreling with God and blaming Him. I had lost my memory during strenuous weeks of trial. I couldn't remember a single verse from the Book by myself. I was dependent on what was printed. I assure you, I would gladly have given not only a fortune *but years of my life if only I could have had that Book*!'

Next morning he begged the Commandant, 'Let me have my Bible back!' The man wavered, but turned to the orderly and said, 'Go and bring the book which is on my desk. It is the Bible. Bring it here!' Niemoller recalls, 'I had not yet been for 12 hours in the concentration camp and the Book entered! The Holy Bible! This Book testifies to the One to whom all power belongs in heaven and earth, even in a concentration camp. There was the Book! And there *He was*, in all His strength, in all His comfort, with all I needed.'*

**PRAYER**
**Do you experience Niemöller's and Daniel's joy in owning a Bible? Then thank Him for this. Ask Him to open your eyes to its riches so you can in turn enrich others as Daniel did. For with the Book comes the God who gave it to us.**

---

*Dr Martin Niemöller at a meeting of the National Bible Society, reported October 1959; taken from *The Message of Daniel* by Ronald S Wallace (IVP).

# 'Bible-Directed Prayer'

**BIBLE READING**
Daniel 9:2–3

**FOCUS VERSE**
'So I turned to the Lord God and pleaded with him in prayer and petition ...' (v.3)

In disturbing times we often don't know what to pray. We're in good company. Even Daniel was clueless, until he found help from the Bible. You must have felt this power too. Daniel studied Jeremiah 25:12–13; 29:10–14 – and *chose to believe it*! Then, as a practical not theoretical student of biblical prophecy – *he prayed it in faith*!

From Jeremiah's predictions, Daniel knew God's countdown to deliverance and restoration was nearing lift off! This meant that *Daniel thought hard about relating God's Word to his own time* (v.2b). He'd been in Babylon nearly 70 years. Babylonian rule ended with Belshazzar's violent overthrow (Dan. 5). Persia came to power after the victory of Darius, who became the new Emperor. Daniel knew God had predicted this, so world events serve God's kingdom and bring blessings to God's people even in exile.

God moves in a mysterious way His wonders to
    perform;
He plants His footsteps in the sea, and rides upon the storm.
Judge not the Lord by feeble sense, but trust Him for
    His grace;
Behind a frowning providence, He hides a smiling face.
**William Cowper (1731–1800)**

Do you look at *our times* – and see God's hand in them? The
men of Issachar '… understood the times and knew what Israel
should do …' (1 Chron. 12:32). The Bible acts like prescription
glasses to help us gain focus and see everything differently,
bringing fresh faith, hope and clarity.

*Daniel cared deeply about what God thought.* He could see
the conditions of God's people deported from home, an ethnic
minority, resident aliens among foes. More importantly, he knew
God cared. We can re-discover this truth that God loves us and
sends the power to recover our fortunes. We can reclaim forgotten
promises that are far from dead, waiting to be mined from
Scripture and believed once again!

*Daniel also knew God was reliable.* If God broke His promises
to us He would have more to lose than we have. We could lose our
lives, but God risks losing His reputation! The God who cannot lie
gave us this Book. Let it find its way into our heads, fire faith and
eager prayer, then trigger our boldest requests of God! Daniel felt
this 'quickening' word. Faith came. He now knew, '*Something great
could happen again … soon!*' Prayer is the reciprocal echo of God's
promises flung back to Him in strong requests to do what He said!

**PRAYER**
**Oh God, our world is in deep trouble too. Show mercy to us
and empower Your people everywhere to believe and bank Your
promissory cheques that pledge revival.**

# 'God-Honouring Prayer'

**BIBLE READING**
Daniel 9:4–6

**FOCUS VERSE**
'O Lord, the great and awesome God,
who keeps his covenant of love ...' (v.4)

*John Calvin devoted 50 pages of his Daniel
commentary to this prayer!* He shows how God
shatters fatalism, apathy and hopeless resignation
to the status quo. God's promises re-attach us to
God's will and God's power. This is how churches
and communities begin to experience renewal
and revival. Renewal affects God's people; revival
impacts their community, city and nation. Here,
Daniel's desperation led to discovery, then strong
desire, certain hope and, finally, divine visitation!
Calvin writes, 'The faithful do not merely relax in
God's promises so as to become torpid, idle or
slothful through the certainty of their persuasion
that God will perform on his promises. Rather, they
are compelled to pray! They ask for what he has
promised. They expect it to happen!'

(1) *Prayer is to be God-centred!* We are not
'contemplating our navel', sitting in the lotus position,
emptying our minds! Daniel's faith didn't rest in the
new government of Persia. He's not awaiting fresh

policies and better laws to save the day. He doesn't want lower taxes and tighter public spending. Instead, He wants God! He wants *God to act! God to move! God to deliver!* The things Daniel lists reveal his awareness of the curses in Deuteronomy 28:15–68. Only God can turn curses back into blessings.

(2) *Prayer is to be passionate and fervent!* Daniel got a grip on his motives and focused his faith. He 'dressed down' in itchy sackcloth to stay awake (v.3). He fasted from food to aid concentration, proving that he meant business. These signs indicate intense mourning over loss, and deep longings for better days! Do you ever 'put yourself out' for desperate prayer? Daniel pours out 'hot' words! He wants God's glory seen and recognised wherever He's been insulted and mocked by bad rulers and wicked men like Nebuchadnezzar or Belshazzar, but supremely seen by God's own people! The heathen were laughing at Daniel's God and His people!

Today, this is due to moribund churches and Christians who misrepresent God and the gospel in the public eye. Daniel couldn't bear this any longer! He prayed for both believers and sceptics to be profoundly affected, saved and restored to their God-ordained humanity and glory!

Are you as desperate as Daniel, eager to experience reversed fortunes and for God's presence to fall on both Church and nation, as it did for the exiles in Babylon? Daniel is not locked up in some private world. He wants God's invasive actions to be seen as real by all.

**PRAYER**
**Lord, my life is often centred on trivia and petty concerns. Wherever I've become distracted and lame in my faith, show me something worthy of my enthusiasm – Your true greatness, and ability to transform nations.**

# 'Honest to God Prayer'

**BIBLE READING**
Daniel 9:4–14

**FOCUS VERSE**
'Lord, you are righteous, but this day we
are covered with shame ... because of our
unfaithfulness to you.' (v.7)

To discover long-desired solutions we must first
acknowledge the real problems. This necessity
directed Daniel's full confession of Israel's true state.

(1) *Daniel owned up to the mess they were
in* (vv.4–10). God is not blamed here, but totally
vindicated by him. Daniel's aware of the shameful
and inexcusable history of Israel that led inevitably
to chastening and exile in Iraq. Much prayer is
simply 'whining to God', full of complaints, venting
anger and frustration that God has let us down:
*'How could You, God? It's not fair!'*

Others resign themselves to the status quo (Latin
for 'The mess we're in'!), declaring piously, 'Well
what can you do? It's up to God. I'm a Calvinist.
God is totally sovereign.' We conclude, 'It's all a total
mystery!' That is rarely the truth. Daniel doesn't blame
the Babylonians. He's not abstract and vague about
his 'culture', the 'atmosphere' or 'the times'. He's
conscious of human responsibility: 'We ...' (v.5),

'We have not listened' (v.6), 'We are covered in shame' (v.7). Ironically, this admission is the pivot for returning hope – 'We' can change!

(2) *Daniel blames himself and his people for their plight, not God* (vv.11–12). Daniel is no 'armchair critic', like the supporter of some run-down Division Two football club mocking from the stands. *Daniel really cares.* The man with unbroken integrity, faithfulness and a fearless refusal to compromise – doesn't blame 'them', or criticise 'that lot' but says, 'us' and 'we' – a mark of his humility and responsibility. This is true 'identificational repentance'! We are *all* to blame!

He calls this a 'great disaster' (v.12b). Daniel loved his nation and people enough to see, face up to and speak the truth. I heard of a boy who fell off his bike and broke his arm. The bone appeared through his skin. His father said, 'Take him away! Take him away! I can't bear to see things like that!' Do you bury your head in sand?

(3) *Daniel doesn't minimise their guilt'* (vv.13–14). He targets his people's true sins. He 'names and shames' for the benefit of all. Deuteronomy 28 makes clear that such sins are guaranteed to 'sink' nations into chaos and divine displeasure, beginning with ancient Israel! Think of our nation's heroin-addicted prostitutes, sexually abused sons and daughters, broken marriages, hardened 'new atheists' penning bestsellers like *The God Delusion* and *God is Not Great*, the temples to strange gods all over Britain, the worship of 'Mammon' in the City. Surely we are all implicated?

**PRAYER**
**Oh God, does this alarm and upset us as it did Daniel? Awaken us and move us to feel as You do about the plight of our nation, and the broken lives of millions in our land. Return to us. Save, heal, reconcile and repair our lives in huge numbers. Use me in any way You choose.**

# 'Revival Faith Prayer'

## BIBLE READING
Daniel 9:14–19

## FOCUS VERSE
'Give ear, O God, and hear; open your eyes and see ... O Lord, listen! O Lord, forgive! O Lord, hear and act!' (vv.18–19)

When nations submit to alien gods and foreign powers, it's a sign they've lost God and forfeited His protection and favour. The evidence is blatant unbelief, blasphemy, soaring crime rates, full prisons, coarse humour, mockery of God, sordid TV programming, the corruption of children's minds, mental breakdown and no moral compass to find our way back.

Even in the Church, God's withdrawal is evident. We see dusty neglected Bibles, dull preaching, poor giving, cold impersonal meetings, dwindling numbers, frayed relationships, ageing congregations, closed church buildings, children and teens turned off the faith!

Like Daniel, we must recover a longing for restoration and revival. When we forfeit blessing and effective mission, it's time to awaken to the reality that we would not be here if we had not sinned. In verses 5–11, Daniel uses a wide Hebrew vocabulary for 'sin': 'missing the mark', 'turning away', 'losing hold on God', 'breach of trust', 'bent minds'. These are clues for the road to recovery. Repentance retraces and renounces the steps we took away from

God, and yearns for the return of God's presence, lost because of:
- our rebellious, wayward spirits (v.5)
- our neglect and ignorance of God's Word (v.5)
- our refusal to hear and heed faithful prophets (v.6a)
- our top-down disobedience to God, from rulers to clerics and pastors and people (v.8)

Few Christians examine such things as our poor giving, 'hearers-only' engagement with preaching, critical spirits, grudges, 'assassination' of godly leaders, worldly talk, and bondage to chronic sinful habits. What would happen if the Church identified and renounced all this before God, as we sought His promised favours again?

To be '*covered with shame*' (vv.7–8) is the beginning of recovery, but this major reversal of fortunes comes from the grace of God in Christ! The Bible teaches everywhere that:
- God's chastening judgments come to an end
- God hears the sincere cries of His people for mercy
- Miraculous reversals can happen suddenly
- We can experience God's presence and glory again!

So Daniel wants God's 'eyes' and 'ears' open to notice their plight (v.18), hear the mocking laughter of the ungodly (v.16), then stir Himself to act and revive their fortunes – '*O Lord, listen! O Lord forgive! O Lord, hear and act … do not delay*' (v.19). Surely, such engaged and fervent revival prayer is the need of the hour for all of us too?

### PRAYER
Lord Jesus, we can't plan for or work up a revival. We can't even organise a successful mission, anointed sermon or a divine healing whenever we want, let alone trigger national recovery and repentance. We call on You, Lord, to do what only God can do. It's time we experienced something great again that will turn our nation back to You. Please start with me.

# Argentina –
# The Businessman
# Turned Evangelist

**W**ithin the history of mission to Latin America,
Argentina was seen as being the most resistant.
A crusade by Tommy Hicks and a subsequent awakening
in the 1950s was the only time of significant church growth
– when many of its neighbours had seen moves of God.

But in the early- to mid-eighties all that changed, and in the
decades which followed, the Protestant Church in Argentina
would know phenomenal growth. It is estimated that in
1990 evangelicals in Argentina numbered half of 1%, roughly
200,000 believers. Today, a minimum of 10% of the population,
or 4 million people, are born again, a 2,000% growth.

Observers of this growth from inside and outside the
revival have offered explanations for this move of God. The
defeat of Argentina by Britain during the Falklands War may
have been a factor. Peter Wagner says: 'The British victory
caused a radical change in Argentine social psychology.
National pride, for which Argentines were internationally
notorious, was severely damaged. The church had failed
them, the military had failed them, Peronism had failed
them – they were ready to try something new.'[1]

Wagner's reference to Peronism is a reminder that there
were those in the leadership of the nation who were hostile

to spiritual growth. In the early 1970s, Juan Domingo Perón linked up with a powerful occult practitioner, José López Rega, known popularly as *el brujo* (the warlock). López Rega served under Perón as social welfare minister, and after Perón's death in 1974 became the chief advisor to his wife, Isabel Perón, during her two years as president. He erected a public monument to witchcraft (since removed) and is said to have publicly cursed the nation when he lost power in the military coup of 1976.

One of today's most knowledgeable Argentine leaders is Edgardo Silvoso of Harvest Evangelism based in San Jose, California. Silvoso ran a workshop at Lausanne II in Manila in 1989 on spiritual warfare in Argentina. There he said:

> If there is one dominant element that has emerged in the
> theology and methodology of evangelism in Argentina,
> I would say it is spiritual warfare. It is an awareness that
> the struggle is not against a political or a social system.
> Nor is it on behalf of those who are captives, but it is
> rather against the jail keepers, against the rulers, those in
> authority in the spiritual realm.[2]

Silvoso contends that understanding this allows Argentine evangelists to get to the root of the problem instead of dealing merely with symptoms.

Observers of the revival, such as Peter Wagner and Ed Silvoso, also note that the revival coincided with the call to evangelism of a Buenos Aires-born businessman, Carlos Annacondia. A descendant of European immigrants (his mother was Spanish and his father of Italian descent), Carlos was born in the city of Quilmes, a province of Buenos Aires on 12 March 1944. He had two brothers and they, as a family, were not wealthy, but later

Carlos opened his own business and became very successful. He married in 1970 and was blessed with nine children.

But Annacondia found that additional homes and cars did not give him the personal peace he sought and he became increasingly concerned about the state of his life, and especially about the future of his children. He attended an evangelistic campaign in the city of San Justo in the province of Buenos Aires on 19 May 1979, curious to see if God was as powerful as people said. The preacher was Manuel A. Ruiz, a pastor from Panama, and Carlos stood at the back of the meeting room. Carlos said that he experienced an 'unmistakable encounter with God, an encounter that impacted me beyond measure. The Holy Spirit touched me in a marvelous way that night.'[3]

Carlos would later write:

> I understood that I was a sinner in need of Him, that I had lived apart from God, in spite of professing the Roman Catholic religion. Indeed, I was, for all intents and purposes, an atheist – a 'Christian atheist' who did not seek God personally, even though I professed to believe in Him. But God came upon me and overcame me that night.

At the back of the meeting room he began to cry. His wife, who was by his side, also began to cry. They were both unable to stop. When the invitation was given they both ran to the front.

From that moment on God began to prepare Carlos for the ministry He had called him into. Deep in his heart, Carlos felt a desire to be an evangelist. He began praying and studying the Bible, and after a year and a half God opened an opportunity for evangelism for him. It was 1981 and he held a series of meetings in a very poor slum area in the city of Bernal. He had no idea what he was doing but was astonished to see how God was moving. Carlos remembers:

God's call to evangelistic ministry began the very
moment I surrendered my life to Christ. I am thankful
that, from the beginning, I had the support and council of
my pastor, Jorge Gomelski. When I was a babe in Christ,
God placed him in my life to disciple me and to teach
me in His ways. I had made a covenant with the Lord. I
promised to serve Him and, in exchange, I asked Him to
give me what the world had promised but was never able
to provide: peace, happiness, security and quietness. All
this God gave me from the moment I committed my life
to Jesus Christ … some have actually come to regard me
as a successful evangelist … it is by His grace alone.[4]

His ministry began among the very poor, in very humble
neighbourhoods, where he would visit hospitals to pray for
the sick. At this time he received a prophecy that he would
start a revival in Argentina, and that, starting from the
southern part of South America, it would spread to the entire
world. Carlos did not dwell on that. His calling from God,
he said, was to preach to the poor and downtrodden. Carlos,
about this time, noticed that when he prayed for the sick they
would be healed. No one was more astonished than he was at
the wonders God was doing through him. Hundreds would
be set free from demonic oppression in the evangelistic
meetings. Ed Silvoso writes: 'The new converts, pouring into
the local churches in record numbers, immediately affected
the spiritual climate of those churches. Through their
dramatic testimonies they became living proof of the power
of God over the power of the devil.'[5]

Annacondia has a great deal in common with traditional
crusade evangelists. He preaches a simple gospel message,
gives an invitation for people to come forward and receive

Christ as their Lord and Saviour, uses trained counsellors to
lead them to Christ and give them literature, takes their name
and address and invites them to attend a local church. Like
Billy Graham and Luis Palau, Annacondia secures a broad
base of interdenominational support from pastors and other
Christian leaders in the target area.

The crusade evangelism approach was seeing fruit as people
responded to Christ, the sick were healed and those oppressed
by demons were set free. Carlos explains how God moved one
extraordinary night:

> In 1992 I got together with 80 local churches to hold
> a big crusade in a northern province. We asked several
> radio and television stations to sell us air time so we
> could broadcast our services live. They all wanted an
> extreme amount of money. More than we could ever
> imagine coming up with. The team was discouraged. So
> we decided to declare spiritual warfare, and we rebuked
> the devil, saying, 'Satan move back. We bind you in the
> name of Jesus. Let go of the means of communication. Go
> away strongman, you are defeated.' We prayed for several
> days. The day before the crusade, we got a call from a
> media executive saying they would sell us the air time
> at 30% less than what they quoted. The FM radio station
> broadcast the crusade at no cost. On Saturday more than
> ten different radio and television stations broadcast the
> service. The first night, five minutes after the beginning
> of the broadcast, the television stations we had not
> contracted with had a technical problem and had to
> discontinue their regular programs. The only thing that
> the entire city could watch that night was our crusade.'[6]

There were reports of thousands being converted that night.

Although he never had the opportunity to attend a seminary or Bible college, or study homiletics or preaching, Annacondia has brought multitudes to Christ, mainly in Argentina, but also in countries such as the United States, Spain, Germany, Russia, Peru, El Salvador, Finland, Puerto Rico, Bolivia, Uruguay and Japan.

Peter Wagner believes the key to Carlos Annacondia's ministry is his intentional, premeditated, high-energy approach to spiritual warfare:

> I have never observed a crusade evangelist who is as publicly aggressive in confronting evil spirits as Annacondia. With a high-volume, high-energy, prolonged challenge he actually taunts the spirits until they manifest in one way or another. To the uninitiated the scenario might appear to be total confusion. But to the skilled, experienced members of Annacondia's 31 crusade ministry teams, it is just another evening of power encounters in which the power of Jesus Christ over demonic forces is being displayed for all to see. Many miraculous healings occur, souls are saved, and so great is the spiritual power that unsuspecting pedestrians passing by the crusade meeting have been known to fall down under the power of the Holy Spirit.[7]

**Notes**

1. Peter Wagner's article on Argentine revival is available at: www.openheaven.com/library/history/argentina.htm
2. Ibid.
3. Taken from article at www.canecreekchurch.org
4. Ibid.
5. Ibid.
6. Ibid.
7. Peter Wagner, op. cit.

1. Do you fast and pray? What value might this have for a church?

2. How would you feel if you had no access to the Bible?

3. The Bible describes a promise-keeping God. When did you last claim one of His promises?

4. Are there any dangers to avoid when claiming a promise?

**5.** What elements of Daniel's praying would you like to incorporate into your prayer life?

**6.** Why do we find it difficult to be honest in private prayer? Why do we find it difficult to be honest in public prayer?

**7.** Has your church been in decline recently? Are there things you need to confess corporately?

**8.** In Argentina's revival God uses an anointed man. What would be the signs that God's hand was on a man or woman? How do you think your church would respond to someone like Carlos Annacondia?

# True Repentance

## By Jonathan Conrathe

## Author Profile

Jonathan Conrathe is the founder and CEO of Valley Life Trust Ltd, which now encompasses Mission24 and Childlife homes: (Mission24.co.uk). He is also the Founding Pastor of City Life Church Telford, UK. He has served in full-time mission work for 23 years in 43 nations. During that time he has been privileged to lead tens of thousands to Christ, and experience the power of God in healing, deliverance, resurrections, and the planting of new churches on four continents. He is married to Elaine and they live in Shropshire, UK with their three boys, Nathan, Joshua and Benjamin.

# Introduction

The first words of both John the Baptist and the Lord Jesus in their public ministries, were, 'Repent, for the kingdom of heaven is at hand!' (Matt. 3:2; 4:17, NKJV). Every move of God, whether in an individual's life, a church, community or nation, begins with a response of repentance when the holiness of God and the sinfulness of man are truly revealed to the human heart. True repentance goes deeper than a change of lifestyle. While it certainly includes that, it affects our entire thinking and value system – it goes to the very root of who we are, and effects a transformation within our character.

Derek Prince once commented, 'without true repentance, there can be no true faith!' – and such faith is so important, for it is the key to the release of the Spirit and miracles in and through our lives (Gal. 3:1–6). Our Father God has an uncompromising purpose to transform us into the image of His Son. That is what the whole creation is groaning for – the revealing of God's sons (Rom. 8:19). In the Western world, many people take issue with 'the Church', but few with Jesus Christ. But when the Church revived thinks, talks, loves and acts like her Lord – an awakening to the reality of His imminent kingdom will be upon us!

# The King is Coming!

**BIBLE READING**
Matthew 3:1–12

**FOCUS VERSE**
'… the kingdom of heaven is at hand!'
(v.2, NKJV)

There had been no clear prophetic voice in Israel for over 400 years and now, suddenly, the thunderous, authentic cry of John the Baptist is heard in the wilderness: 'Repent, for the kingdom of heaven is at hand [imminent]!' (Matt. 3:2). Without the 'now Word' of God, the 'Rhema' which we hear through intimate seasons with God, our lives can become swamped with the daily issues of life, and all sense of identity with Christ and His destiny upon our lives somehow 'dulled' by the demands of this world. The Scriptures were given to lead us into a believing relationship with the One of Whom they testify (John 20:30–31), and the ministry of God is to be Spirit and Life, not 'dead letter'! The word of repentance is a 'wake up' call, a cry to re-align ourselves with heaven's realities … 'The kingdom, or reign, of God is at hand …!'

In days gone by, when royalty was to visit a certain town or city, messengers would be sent ahead to herald the coming of the king. The response was often dramatic as great preparations would ensue, roads were repaired, and everything about people's daily lives generally sharpened up and brought into order. The king was coming. His royalty, his culture, was imposed upon the prevailing culture of the day, and it would bring change! The kingdom of God has come through Christ, is here by the power of His Holy Spirit, and will be manifested in fullness at His return in power and glory. The transformation that His kingdom accomplishes *in* us when we receive Jesus as our Lord and Saviour and start to become renewed in our minds to think as He does (Rom. 12:1–2), must also start to effect change in the lives and communities *around* us. The accusation levied against the early apostles was 'these men who have turned the world upside down have come here also' (Acts 17:6, ESV)! If we will not allow Jesus to turn *our* lives upside down, what hope do we have of impacting anyone else's?

The question we have to ask ourselves today is 'Do we stand out, or do we merely blend in?' Does our light really shine and penetrate the darkness because our relationship with Jesus is shining brightly through our attitudes, words and deeds, or are we allowing our enemy to dull the light and its impact through a preoccupation with ourselves? The call to Christ-likeness is both moral and missional. He who commanded 'Love one another as I have loved you', also commanded 'Heal the sick … and tell them the kingdom of God has drawn near you.'

**PRAYER**
**Lord, at the beginning of this week, I surrender myself afresh, I want to realign myself with You, and the purposes of Your kingdom, that Your reign might be revealed *in* and *through* my life to a world desperate for the love and power of God.**

# Blessed are Those who Hunger

**BIBLE READING**
Matthew 3:1–12

**FOCUS VERSE**
'People went out to him from Jerusalem and all Judea and the whole region of the Jordan.' (v.5)

In the autumn of 2005, Hurricane Katrina crashed into the shores of the USA causing untold damage that is still being cleared today. However, before it reached the shores of America, it had already taken its toll on Mexico, leaving tens of thousands homeless within a 6km radius of its epicentre. In the middle of that catastrophic situation, we were conducting a mission. To make a long story short, a desperate woman had brought her nine-year-old crippled son to the meetings. She had once walked with God, but had married a non-Christian and gone away from the Lord for a number of years. Their son had a degenerative condition in his hip and the right leg had stopped growing. Now, his only hope for mobility was a large built-up shoe secured with callipers round his leg. His mother heard our broadcast inviting the sick to come to the mission, and she made a commitment to the Lord that if He would heal her son, she would follow Him for the rest of her life. It took her several hours to wade through water, fallen trees and other such obstacles, but both she and multitudes of onlookers wept and rejoiced as the boy's leg straightened and grew out in front of everyone in response to the spoken word of God. She was desperate, she was willing to take a risk of faith, she was rewarded. Blessed are those who hunger! (Matt. 5:6).

True repentance and faith bring us into a place where our convictions become firmly rooted in the Word of God, and our expectation is determined more by a revelation of truth than by the nature of our circumstances. When we act on that truth, we position ourselves for the miraculous interventions of God! Hunger and thirst for any aspect of God's kingdom is preceded by a conviction of God's power and goodness, and that He will do what He promises! Furthermore, it empowers the kind of faith that perseveres until it possesses what has been promised (Heb. 6:11–12). Jesus told a story about a woman who finally obtained justice for herself from an unjust judge because of her relentless persistence in coming to him for vindication (Luke 18:1–8). He compared this to the believer's prayer life, but ended with the challenging statement 'when the Son of Man comes, will he find faith on the earth?' Sometimes we give up too soon. It's too easy to lose our inheritance through complacency and then develop a stronghold in our thinking by justifying our situation with some doctrine about the sovereignty of God! Jesus said, 'Everyone who asks [and keeps asking, Gk] receives ...' (Luke 11:9–10). The famous Argentinian evangelist, Ed Silvoso, is noted for saying 'a stronghold is a mindset which causes us to accept as unchangeable things that we know are contrary to the will of God'. Today, let's move beyond disappointments in our history to embrace a destiny in the kingdom of God.

**PRAYER**
**Father God, help me to apply the truth of Your Word to the strongholds in my thinking until I become fully persuaded and embrace with perseverance the promises of God. I shall possess my inheritance!**

# Show Me Your Faith!

**BIBLE READING**
Matthew 3:1–12

**FOCUS VERSE**
'Produce fruit in keeping with repentance.' (v.8)

Amongst the multitudes who came out to hear the powerful preaching of John the Baptist and repent of their sins, were the religious leaders of the day. While John clearly welcomed the sincere repentance of the masses, his response to the Pharisees and Sadducees was nothing less than scathing! His blistering statements bring into sharp focus that God cannot countenance religious hypocrisy. Neither spiritual heritage nor any form of godliness (lacking the substance of real power to change lives) makes any positive impression on the heart of God. He is looking for fruit! 2 Corinthians 5:17 declares 'if anyone is in Christ, he is a new creation; old things have passed away; behold, all things have become new' (NKJV). Essentially, when we receive Christ, the real person that we are, the 'hidden man of the heart' as Peter called him, becomes a new person, a new creation. In Greek, the word 'new' in this context does not refer to new in terms of 'time' but in terms of substance or quality. Literally, a new life, God's own Divine Nature (1 Pet. 1:23) has been imparted to our hearts and we have become 'alive to God'! The result: the old things that surrounded the old life pass away, and all things become new. The root determines the fruit.

In his letter, the apostle James further addresses this issue, saying 'faith ... if it is not accompanied by action, is dead' (James 2:17). While we are not saved *by* good works, we are certainly saved *for* them ... (Eph. 2:9–10), and the fruit of a life lived for God, demonstrating His love, purity and power, is evidence that a new life has truly been imparted to us by the Word and Spirit of God.

The dangers of hypocrisy are very real. The word itself originally came from Greek theatre life where an actor would pick up a mask to cover his face and take on another persona. If we are going to bring glory to our heavenly Father by bearing much fruit through a life-giving union with Christ (John 15:1–8), we have to lay down all pretence and all excuses for our attitudes and behaviour and allow the Lord to deal with the reality of our hearts and lives. When helping those with various addictions, I have had to say to them, 'if you lie to me, we part company ... no one can help a liar, because Truth is the freeing agent!' But when we bring to the light the issues that have been in darkness, we can be truly cleansed (1 John 1:7). But it goes much further than that – God's intention is that we move from active sin to passionate righteousness, from passive unbelief to positive faith. When we truly believe, our faith will not only lead us into right behaviour but into fruitful ministry to others. Our actions of faith will become conduits of God's power and compassion to those in need. It was when the crippled beggar (Acts 3) arose that his ankles received strength (Gk, *Dunamis*: power), when Moses lifted his rod that the seas parted, and when Peter stepped out of the boat that he walked on water.

**PRAYER**
**Heavenly Father, I choose today to not be a 'forgetful hearer'**
**of God's Word, but a 'doer' of it, and to see the reality of Christ's**
**kingdom released through my life.**

# The Purifying Power of Confession

**BIBLE READING**
Matthew 3:1–12

**FOCUS VERSE**
'Confessing their sins, they were baptised by him in the Jordan River.' (v.6)

The nature of light is that it exposes what is in darkness. The preaching of John the Baptist powerfully exposed the darkness of sin in the hearts of his hearers, leading to conviction, confession and repentance expressed in water baptism.

Thank God for confession! It gives us the opportunity to come clean with God and be freed from the sins we have committed. It enables us to move on with God into a positive and productive future. I recall, during a mission service we conducted in South America, that at the end of the message the Holy Spirit instructed me to express that there was a man in the building who had been committing adultery, that his wife knew nothing about it, but that God was calling him to repentance. Suddenly, the doors at the back of the hall flung open, and a man who had been cleaning the offices in the rear of the building came running to the front and fell into the arms of the pastors, confessing, 'I'm the man!' He wept in repentance, committed his life to Christ and was restored that night to his wife. Four years later that man departed from this life into the welcoming arms of His Saviour, and around his bedside stood his family and his many relatives all of whom he had led to Christ following his conversion that night. Confession is part and parcel of repentance. It involves the humility to acknowledge before God, and sometimes to a trusted brother or sister (James 5:16), that we have sinned. In the words of Charles Finney,

> Repentance implies an intellectual and hearty giving up
> of all controversy with God upon all and every point.
> It implies a conviction that God is wholly right, and
> the sinner is wholly wrong, and a thorough and hearty
> abandonment of all excuses and apologies for sin.

'… if anyone sins, we have an advocate with the Father, Jesus Christ the righteous. And he himself is the propitiation for our sins …' (1 John 2:1, NKJV). Thank God there is forgiveness and cleansing as often as we need it! However, let us note today that this verse begins with the word 'if'. While in His goodness, the Lord has provided ongoing forgiveness for the believer through the blood of Christ, His heart, in the words of Arthur Wallis, was that confession would be the emergency exit, not the daily staircase! There is grace for forgiveness, but thank God there is also grace for victory. Grace is a word of pardon and power. Today, if you need to do so, get on your knees and confess your sins to your Father in heaven, and do so with the confidence that 'He is faithful and just to forgive our sins and cleanse us from ALL unrighteousness'.

### PRAYER
Father God, I pray for Your empowering grace to strengthen my decision to turn from sin, that I might forget the past and move forward with my eyes firmly fixed on You. I would keep saying 'Yes' to Jesus. I know that He who called me is faithful, and He will complete the work He's begun in me.

# Filled with Power

**BIBLE READING**
Matthew 3:1–12

**FOCUS VERSE**
'He will baptise you with the Holy Spirit and with fire' (v.11)

I had been preaching around the Southern counties of England on the necessity of being 'baptised in the Holy Spirit', and a young boy of just nine years old came to me, asking to be filled with the power of the Spirit. He had already given his life to Christ, but as was true of the believers in Samaria, he had not yet received the Holy Spirit (Acts 8:14–17). As I told him that when I laid hands on him he would be filled with the Spirit, his thirst for God was very evident (I have learned from the experience of praying for thousands of people to receive the Holy Spirit that very often the level of our thirst determines the level of our experience!). I rested my hand on him to begin praying but, before I could get a word out of my mouth, he burst forth in other tongues. Jesus said, 'If anyone is thirsty, let him come to Me and drink. He who believes in Me, as the Scripture said, "From his innermost being will flow rivers of living water!"' (John 7:37–39, NASB). Jesus is still today (Heb. 13:8) the 'Baptiser in the Holy Spirit!' (John 1:33).

The commands of Jesus are not only moral, they are also missional. In the great commission, the first disciples were told to go and, amongst other things, teach those who believed in Christ to observe all things that He commanded them. His commands include: 'preach, saying, "The kingdom of heaven is at hand." Heal the sick, cleanse the lepers, raise the dead, cast out demons' (Matt. 10:8, NKJV). However, to accomplish such kingdom acts, we first need kingdom power, and that's where the Holy Spirit comes in. Jesus said, 'you will receive power when the Holy Spirit comes on you; and you will be my witnesses ...' (Acts 1:8).

I have a good friend in the Philippines who, following his conversion, was frustrated in his lack of results when sharing the gospel. He determined that he would go into his hut, close the door and pray until he received the power he needed. Three days in, he heard the sounds of the locals outside throwing water to put out the fire that they could see on the top of his hut, but it was not physical fire, it was a manifestation of the Holy Spirit. My friend was filled with the Spirit, started speaking in other tongues and worshipping God, and from then on he and his team went on to plant over one hundred churches across the Philippines through the power of God. Are you thirsty? Come to Him, ask, receive in faith and be filled with the Holy Spirit, not only once, but again, and again, and again, and become a life-changing witness to Christ in your world!

## PRAYER
**Lord, I would thirst for You more and more. I come now and ask You to fill me with Your Holy Spirit that I might truly be a life-changing witness to Christ, that I might show Him to the world around me.**

# Mozambique – Heidi Baker

Mozambique is known as a country that has faced desperate hardship, even by African standards. It suffered a civil war from 1977 to 1992, and a cyclone and devastating floods in early 2000, leaving an already impoverished country with many orphaned, poorly fed and with little hope of education and a future. Disease, poor nutrition and scarce medical facilities mean life expectancy is just 48. Economists rate it as one of the poorest countries in Africa.

It was to this land that God called Heidi Baker, and in this nation that God has been at work.

Missionaries since 1980, Heidi and husband Rolland arrived in Mozambique in 1995 having served among the poor in Thailand, Hong Kong and England.

Heidi had been called as a missionary in 1975 when she was sixteen and living in southern California. She recalls the story in her book *Compelled by Love*:

> A bright white light surrounded me, and I heard an
> external, audible voice from God for the first time in my
> life. I was sixteen years old. Jesus told me that I was to be
> married to Him. Oil ran down my arm, and I felt Him

kiss my left ring finger. He said, 'You are called to be a minister and a missionary. You are called to Africa, Asia, and England.' When the heavy, weighty presence of God lifted, I was alone in the church. I had been motionless with my hands raised for nearly three hours.[1]

God's assurance that He would work in Mozambique was no less dramatic. Heidi recalls:

I had gone to this huge church, trying to hide in the back and be incognito. I really wasn't supposed to be there, but I wanted to hear this man [Randy Clark] preach. He was preaching about the fire of God, the anointing of God, and the hunger and thirst to give your life away for God, and I remember the message being so powerful that I couldn't wait for the altar call. The truth is, I'm a bit shy in the natural. So I wanted to be good and listen to the rules, not just push my way forward when the time came. But I just couldn't stand it! I stood up from the middle of the back row I was in and immediately ran forward, screaming the whole way. I was really shocked at myself. Randy Clark, who was preaching, never hesitated. He laid his hands on me and said, 'Do you want the nation of Mozambique? The blind will see. The crippled will walk. The deaf will hear. The dead will be raised, and the poor will hear the good news.' I screamed, 'Yes!' Then I was wholly undone, totally wrecked. When I say wrecked, I mean being completely under the heavy, weighty glory of God. I wasn't able to walk for days. People had to carry me. I felt the power of God pulsating through me. It was truly awesome. I have never recovered from that day![2]

This word from God has come true to the letter. Heidi's books recount the way God has used her and her husband to reach the poor, set up schools, plant churches and transform communities in Mozambique – part of an extraordinary movement of God in that country.

In 2002, they left a flourishing ministry among orphans in the south of Mozambique to locate to Pemba, a small town of some 50,000 people in the province of Cabo Delgado on the northeast coast. The predominant Makua people group was considered virtually unreached and unreachable. Missiologists reported at the time that the Makua was one of the most unreached people groups in sub-Saharan Africa. When Heidi and Rolland first moved to Pemba, there were very few missionaries living there. She was immediately able to lead 15 people to Jesus who when they turned up at the first discipleship meeting were still manifesting demons. Every week Heidi and her husband would drive out into the darkness in their Land Rover full of singing children, and preach the good news of salvation in Jesus' name. And every week there were miracles.

Today there are hundreds and hundreds of churches among the Makua, and thousands have put their faith in Jesus. As Heidi says: 'God continually performs mighty deeds through the meek and humble who love Him.'

They were able to plant a second church at Mieze village 20 minutes' drive west of Pemba. This has developed into a forerunner for other churches across the province, which now number more than 1,700. The Mieze church has become more than a simple mud hut with meetings on Sunday. It has become a modest prototype of community development and transformation. The holy Presence of God is manifested here in a beautiful kaleidoscope of ways, including healings that the people have come to expect, and receive regularly.

'The Presence' in the bush of Africa also looks like homes, schools, farms, food, water wells, family, adoption of many children, fellowship, miracles, fun – the full spectrum of life in God! Out of isolation, paganism and witchcraft have risen a people given over to Jesus.

The miracles did not always come quickly. Heidi prayed for the blind for a year and was not getting good results. She was in a little mud hut church when a lady who was blind approached her. This little beggar lady's eyes were completely white. As Heidi held this lady in her arms, God completely transformed her with His glory, and she fell to the ground and began to scream. As Heidi watched her eyes, they began to turn from white to grey and then to brown. She could see! Everyone around started yelling and screaming, 'Mama Aida can see! Mama Aida can see!' In Mozambique, Heidi's own name was also Mama Aida.

Shortly after this, Heidi saw a lady in her 30s who had been blind since she was eight years old. Again, it was as Heidi held the woman and felt God's heart of love for her, that she began to scream, 'You're wearing a black shirt!' She could see! When Heidi took her outside into the light, the other villagers heard her screams, and they too began to scream, 'Mama Aida can see! Mama Aida can see!' The first two ladies whom she ever prayed for who received their sight, both had Heidi's Mozambique name.

During the season of Ramadan, one of the unreached groups of people announced on the radio, 'We are losing the battle to Ministrrio Arco-Iris [Iris Ministries, Heidi's organisation]. We cannot keep up with them,' they said. 'They feed the poor, take in orphans, the dead are being raised, the blind see, the crippled walk, and the deaf hear. We are losing the battle.'

When asked what their strategic plan is – Heidi and Rolland laugh. God's plan was simple – for them to stop what they were doing and go to the poor, sit with them and learn to love them. So this is what they did – not with the intention of starting a church growth movement but to learn about the kingdom from the poor and the children as they sat with them in the street.

Heidi writes:

> Later, blind eyes started to see, deaf ears started to hear, those who had crippled limbs started to walk, and the poor local pastors in their mud huts started to raise the dead. Now in Mozambique we have seen more than one hundred people raised from the dead! The people bring the dead in their coffins to our street preachers and our bush preachers. They bring babies who have died, and sometimes they live again in Jesus's name![3]

Iris Ministries currently feeds well over 10,000 children a day, as well as various members of many other communities, currently including 4,000 families in Malawi. Its network of churches also numbers more than 10,000, including some 2,000 churches among the Makua people of northern Mozambique. Iris operates five Bible schools, in addition to its three primary schools and its school of missions in Pemba.

Mozambique is believed to have had the fastest church growth of any Black African country in the 1990s.

## Further Reading

Heidi Baker with Rolland Baker, *There is Always Enough* (Grand Rapids, MI: Chosen Books, 2003).

Heidi Baker with Rolland Baker, *The Hungry Always Get Fed* (Bognor Regis, West Sussex: New Wine Press, 2007).

Heidi Baker with Rolland Baker, *Expecting Miracles: True Stories of God's Supernatural Power and How You Can Experience It* (Grand Rapids, MI: Chosen Books, 2007).

Heidi Baker with Shara Pradhan, *Compelled By Love* (Lake Mary, FL: Charisma House, 2008).

**Notes**
1. Heidi Baker, *Compelled by Love* (Lake Mary, FL: Charisma House, 2008). Used by permission.
2. Ibid.
3. Ibid.

1. Do you stand out or blend in? In your daily life, where might there be opportunities to stand for Christ which you are currently not taking?

2. Ed Silvoso, is noted for saying 'a stronghold is a mindset which causes us to accept as unchangeable things that we know are contrary to the will of God.' Can you think of things you had assumed were not going to change, but which really should?

3. Why is hypocrisy such a big deal for God?

**4**. 'Confession is to be an emergency exit, not a daily staircase'. How would you help someone who finds themselves confessing the same sins every week?

**5**. Most churches in the UK do not have the same power that we see in the book of Acts. Why do you think this is?

**6**. Heidi Baker prayed for a year for the blind without seeing any results. It is not uncommon for many to see a breakthrough in prayer after much persistence. How quickly do you give up praying for something that is not happening?

# God is Always Ready!

**By Gerald Coates**

## Author Profile

Gerald Coates is best known as a speaker, author and broadcaster. He has addressed well over one million people face to face, has written ten books, and has taken part in numerous programmes for BBC1 and ITV television, as well as BBC radio. He hosted a chat show on Christian television and was featured in a documentary called *Handfuls of Heaven* on ITV. He founded the Pioneer network of Churches, training programmes and ministries. He has been married to Anona for 45 years. They have three grown-up sons and three grandchildren. He is team leader of Pioneer Engage Church in Leatherhead, Surrey.

# Introduction

Revival! The very word can thrill individuals and communities with passion and prayer. Stories can be told about South Korea, China, North India, South America, and massive events where in several days over one million people believe in Jesus, receive the Holy Spirit, signing cards and giving names.

For others, revival has become a word acquainted with unfulfilled expectations. News addicts and those disillusioned with the Church are high on the list of these. They are more in touch with earth than they are with heaven.

However, I have been privileged to speak to tens of thousands in Uganda, witnessed a short-lived revival in Nashville where people were queuing up an hour or more before the meeting. And I am a keen observer of revival history in Wales and Sunderland, as well as the recent growth of some black majority and other key churches in major cities in the UK.

And as you read this, remember, 'God's Spirit is on me'. Christ's revival Spirit is on the largest growing people movement around the world – the Church. The Church has never been as large or growing as fast as it is now. What is your part in this?

# The Revival Spirit

**BIBLE READING**
Luke 4:16–34

**FOCUS VERSE**

'God's Spirit is on me;
  he's chosen me to preach the Message of
    good news to the poor,
Sent me to announce pardon to prisoners and
  recovery of sight to the blind,
To set the burdened and battered free,
  to announce, "This is God's year to act!"'
(v.18, *The Message*)

As exciting as this verse is, the personal application of it may mean different things to different people.

He cried – he tried not to, but he couldn't help himself, he was overwhelmed. It was a gathering of leaders from around the UK. There had been the usual time of contemporary worship. Now it was the time for the speaker.

He walked to the podium, opened his Bible to Luke chapter 4 verse 16. First there was the faltering voice, then he choked up, he couldn't speak. Pressing on, tears began to flow and suddenly the hotel room full of leaders realised that although these words were indeed the words of Christ, he was applying them to himself, 'God's Spirit is on me'.

Later I was to discover that as he went to read this passage he became aware of a DVD playing in his mind, of his youthful, sexual promiscuity, of his cover-ups, dishonesty and opinionated positions which drew some people into his affections and kept many others out. He was also aware of how proud he was of his biblical knowledge. In his eyes, he was sexually filthy, academically arrogant and unforgiving.

But the fact is, as a young man I too was sexually curious and promiscuous, even as a 'believer', employing cover-up tactics that became more sinful than the original wrongdoing. The public Gerald Coates was a very different person to the private Gerald Coates.

As the great atheist turned Christian, Malcolm Muggeridge, told me, 'The trick, my dear boy, is to keep your public life as close to your private life as possible – otherwise these two people will be barely on a nodding acquaintance with each other.' And how right he was.

The pure, powerful, holy, clean, forgiving, creative, intelligent, supernatural Spirit of God is on wrongdoers, liars, cheats and impure people like you and me! It's unbelievable. As Bill Johnson says, 'He is in you for yourself, on you for others'.

And then Christ goes on to say that the outworking of this is good news for the poor and powerless, pardon to wrongdoers, healing for the sick, and freedom for those imprisoned by history and abuse.

Are you ready?

**PRAYER**
**Dear Lord, I thank You for grace and mercy, and for the shed blood of Christ, allowing You to place Your Holy Spirit in me and on me. I humble myself before You and reaffirm my commitment to You. Amen.**

# The Spirit and Humanity!

**BIBLE READING**
Luke 4:16–34

**FOCUS VERSE**

'All who were there, watching and listening, were surprised at how well he spoke. But they also said, "Isn't this Joseph's son, the one we've known since he was a youngster?"'
(v.22, *The Message*)

To bring this passage to life I would like to use a very personal illustration.

I have spoken at March For Jesus, Spring Harvest, The Royal Albert Hall, Wembley Arena and Stadium, The Berlin Stadium, and major events in Canada, America, Germany, Uganda and other places. Yet, invitations to speak in my 'home town' have been few.

Maybe my experience is similar to that of Jesus – perhaps God is teaching me from the same truth that we see in Scripture that a prophet is not without value, honour or indeed respect except in his own patch?

Jesus devoured Scripture, was deeply and personally related to His heavenly Father, and yet people nevertheless were 'surprised' at His education, knowledge of Scripture and theological creativity. Why? They had grown up with Him. To them He was merely 'Joseph's son'.

So what is the lesson? Family or local people may not realise your education, your value in the workplace or in your wider field of influence perhaps because they do not recognise that God's Spirit is on you. But that is not important. If it is genuinely God's Spirit on you, God does. Just as Jesus' Father knew who He was, what He had done, and what He was about to do. We have to live before God, not merely men and women.

Again to quote Malcolm Muggeridge, 'Always let people underestimate you, it gets a lot of fun as you grow older!' In other words, people may well write you off because of a lack of education, youthfulness or old age, social background or financial situation, but when God's Spirit is upon you it is surprising where God will take you and what He will do in and through you. There is no need to trumpet achievements, because God is a great bookkeeper, He writes it all down and is actually going to reward us for what we should have done in the first place!

What a God!

**PRAYER**
**Dear Lord, save me from ever feeling sorry for myself, if perhaps I'm feeling that my ministry doesn't receive the recognition I think it should. Keep me in prayer, for I know that You can do what I cannot and that it is You I am serving. Amen.**

# Revival Squashed

## BIBLE READING
Luke 4:16–34

## FOCUS VERSES

'No prophet is ever welcomed in his hometown.
Isn't it a fact that there were many widows in Israel
at the time of Elijah during that three and a half
years of drought when famine devastated the land,
but the only widow to whom Elijah was sent was
in Sarepta in Sidon? And there were many lepers in
Israel at the time of the prophet Elisha but the only
one cleansed was Naaman the Syrian.'
(vv.24–25, *The Message*)

In one sense, these are difficult sayings. However,
Christ was talking about a situation where there
can be pain and suffering despite a prophet being
present. Indeed, just as it was in His day. There are
many people today who are spiritually blind, who are
not ready for Christ or what He has to offer. Jesus
of course knew this. Despite our views of heaven
and hell, one does not get the impression that Christ
is rushing around the Middle East looking for every
opportunity to stop people going to an eternity
without Christ.

This raises many theological questions; because
Christ is our model of theology, our understanding of
God His Father, ecclesiology (the way we do Church)
and eschatology (end time issues). But Christ did
believe in judgment and hell. In fact, on over 20

occasions He mentions hell as a place of darkness, suffering and separation from God.

The story now changes. Their initial amazement turns to hostility, taking exception that somebody they knew, 'Joseph's son', was making incredible claims for Himself. They demand visible proof. Enraging them further, Christ explains that when prophets in Israel had been faced with disbelief and cynicism they performed their miracles outside Israel (1 Kings 17:8–16; 2 Kings 5:1–14). Christ's words of grace and promise have now turned to judgment. This was the first suggestion that the gospel would ultimately go to far more Gentiles (non-Jewish people) than the Jews themselves.

They were so angry that they tried to kill Him.

We are a people of grace and promise. Ultimate judgment is in the hands of God, even though we have to make judgments on a daily basis.

But just imagine what could have happened if they had searched the Scriptures, had their eyes opened and honoured the greatest prophet of all time! Revival?

**PRAYER**
**Dear Lord, thank You for allowing the gospel to break out of the life of Christ, the Jewish community and down throughout the centuries to reach me – what would I have been without You? Amen.**

# Revival Continues

## BIBLE READING
Luke 4:16–34

## FOCUS VERSES

> 'He went down to Capernaum, a village in Galilee. He was teaching the people on the Sabbath. They were surprised and impressed – his teaching was so forthright, so confident, so authoritative, not the quibbling and quoting they were used to.'
> (vv.31–32, *The Message*)

I often wonder whether the religious leaders Christ left behind were aware of which direction He was now going in. Capernaum! It was almost as though He were brushing the dust off His feet and walking away from those who not only could not hear but were trying to silence Him. Instead, He returns to the place where He had been heard and seen for who He was. The religious leaders knew this was Capernaum.

And when He arrived and began teaching He spoke with such clarity that His listeners were surprised.

We live in an age where even amongst Evangelicals there is little intentional evangelism. There is plenty of social action, prayer, seed sowing, children's and youth work. But the gospel barely gets a mention. 'We'll tell them if they ask' as one youth worker put it to me.

We, the Church, swing between declaration and demonstration. There was a time when we were all words. We were out on the streets with our banners and megaphones trying to get into school assemblies to preach the gospel, and of course there were listeners and responders. But most were put off. We realised we had to demonstrate we cared for these people, so we opened up youth clubs, gave help to the poor and got lost in a myriad of activities. Then the gospel got lost and we swung back to declaration. To be biblically balanced we need to hold these two things in tension.

Elsewhere, Dr Luke tells us that Jesus was a doer as well as a teacher (Acts 1:1) and no doubt His doing (demonstration) caused people to listen to His teaching (declaration). And they responded to His clarity, confidence and authority. His was the big, broad and wonderful picture of God and His empire, not the legalism, the small-mindedness or the rights and wrongs of being a good Jew. The latter they were used to, and had tuned out and turned off.

It is wonderful when churches bring their own strengths to a community, demonstrating love and kindness but also speaking with clarity and authority.

We actually need to be Good News. This invariably allows us to share who we are and why we do what we do. So it's good news for everybody.

**PRAYER**
**Thank You, dear Lord, that Your gospel is one of Word and deed. Help me to demonstrate and declare in equal measure and to keep these in tension. Amen.**

# Recognition Arrives

## BIBLE READING
Luke 4:16–34

## FOCUS VERSES

'In the meeting place that day, there was a man demonically disturbed. He screamed, "Ho! What business do you have here with us, Jesus? Nazarene! I know what you're up to. You're the Holy One of God and you've come to destroy us!"' (vv.33–34, *The Message*)

I find it amazing that people who knew the Scriptures, taught them and instructed others, should fail to recognise the One for whom Israel was waiting. However, it seems the demonic world is often more perceptive than we humans.

Christ was teaching in the synagogues when the congregations met on the Sabbath. On this occasion a demoniac was present. Today he would probably be seen as suffering from a mental illness or some other handicap. However, this would be an incorrect diagnosis.

Just as we recognise that the Holy Spirit works through people's words and actions, we must recognise that evil spirits are at work in some of those around us.

This man had incredible insight into the name of Jesus and His mission in life. He describes Him as 'the Holy One of God', which linguists point out means much the same as Son of God or Christ.

It has been noted that the demoniac may have thought he could overpower Jesus by using His name – this was a common superstition in those days. Instead, Christ commands the demon to leave the man. This confirmed even further the impression of the remarkable authority which Christ's teaching had already given His listeners.

As a result of minds being revived through Christ's teaching, and hearts being revived through His care, the demoniac is revived, moving from darkness to light, from disorder to order. Christ silenced the demoniac because He wanted people to learn and to see who He was for themselves.

However, despite His idolisation and reception, He refused to become a star of His day and therefore did not stay long enough in one place to become trapped by the admiring throng.

So it can be with us. Let us go and speak to the crowds or the ones and twos where we know God has called us to go. He will move through the power of His Spirit, whether that be to many or a few. But these places can become unsafe if we draw too much comfort from them. Like Christ, we have a mission in life; it is not to go round in circles but to progress on a revival journey with a purpose.

**PRAYER**
**Dear Lord, Give us eyes to see what we need to see, and teach us how to walk in Your authority against dark forces that surround Your people. Amen.**

# India – The Welsh Connection

Almost exactly 100 years after a revival in Meghalaya, northeast India, God moved again in a powerful way. Welsh missionaries, empowered by the awakening in Wales in 1904 had brought the gospel to northeast India and seen significant results. Following an initial awakening in February 1905, it was reported that by 1906 the Khasi Revival brought in an estimated 4,000. Others say that the church saw 8,200 former Hindus baptised within two years.

In 2003, local Christians in the Khasi Jaintia Presbyterian Synod (West) in Meghalaya began praying in earnest that God would again bring revival, as they anticipated the anniversary of the awakening of 1905–06 and longed that God would visit them. They began an ongoing chain prayer movement and opened the doors of the chapel every morning to give opportunity for prayer that God would reverse the spiritual decline among His Church. Other denominations shared this burden and soon there was fervent and heartfelt longing for God to visit them again. All the seven northeastern states have a significant population of Christians and at least three states in the region – Meghalaya, Mizoram and Nagaland – have a Christian majority.

Mathew Backholer, a writer and broadcaster who is an expert on revival, reports that:

> The revival began on Saturday the 22 April 2006 among a huge number of people in Mairang, the place where the 1906 revival first broke out. Hundreds of delegates were attending the afternoon service of the Revival Centenary commemoration, whilst a minimum of 150,000 people (with reports of up to 300,000) sat outside on the huge lawns of the Mairang Presbyterian Church. The Holy Spirit came 'in such a powerful way' that the delegates continued to sing and pray for hours, unmoved, in driving rain which continued for about half an hour, oblivious to the elements.[1]

Barkos Warjri, a Khasi who lives in Shillong, wrote:

> The revival is taking place in area of about 14,000 square kilometres and has affected thousands of local churches. The churches affected have been almost entirely Presbyterian but a few other denominations have been touched.[2]

The revival has even touched some churches in the adjoining state of Mizoram. Warjri continues:

> Many people, especially children have been miraculously converted without any preaching, but simply by the conviction of the Holy Spirit. Miraculous events have also taken place in many of the churches with thousands of children throughout the hills seeing visions of God, Jesus Christ, heaven, hell, resulting in convictions of

these children, their relatives or the churches concerned.
Families and whole communities have been transformed.[3]

The Holy Spirit even descended on 'all schools in the area,
be they state schools, church schools, or private schools [and
on a college of more than two thousand pupils!] For several
of the schools, regular classes were disrupted. Children from
the age of about five expressed strong desires to be in church
or simply to sing praises to God and pray.'[4]

Such was the supposed veracity of these claims, the news
story appeared on the BBC news website on 1 October 2006.

At one state school, the Holy Spirit descended and the effect
on the teenagers, all of whom were in their smart school
uniforms, was caught on video. Backholer writes:

I have seen the footage. Some were worshiping the Lord,
sitting on the desks, kneeling or standing, whilst others
were crying, still others were in prayer, and some were
even being carried out of the classrooms in what I would
call a spiritual comatose state, being under the power of
the Holy Spirit.[5]

An American missionary wrote of the revival:

I first witnessed this happening on 30th May 2006 when
we went for a Bible study in one village near the town of
Shillong, in a small Presbyterian church in Lumthehsei
Umroi. Mr Khlainbor Lyngdoh had given the Bible study
and started praying for the people and giving the altar
call; people started praying together and the anointing of
the Holy Spirit swept the place in such an amazing way
and people without even laying of hands were falling in
the Spirit ... and we were all filled with the Spirit of God

and the service which usually lasts 2 hours went on and on with praying and singing that no one left the church even till the wee hours of the morning.

I did not realize then that this manifestation of the Power of the Holy Spirit was going to sweep the whole State of Meghalaya in a matter of few months.

This was happening in every Bible study we went to and it was an amazing experience since we were working mostly in the rural parts of Meghalaya. After a few months in a MIGHTY wave the Spirit swept not only in rural areas but in the main capital of the State in town, in Churches/in homes/Schools/Colleges and at most times classes had to be stopped and closed for the day as even in Schools and Colleges children were singing and praying. They were taking their Bibles/Hymnals to school and sharing there, thus inviting the Holy Spirit and a Revival swept the place with children and youth sleeping in the Spirit sometimes even for days without food and water, but when asked they say that Jesus used to feed them with fruits and something like fruit juices ... This wave of the Spirit was mostly among children below 15 years and the youths, to fulfil the Word of God in Joel 2:18. It was like experiencing what the disciples of Jesus experienced in the Day of Pentecost in Acts 1 and 2.[6]

Friday Lyngdoh, Minister with the Meghalaya Government, in January 2007 said that the changes in society were real. When asked if he had seen any of the big signs of the revival, he replied, 'No, I have not. But I have seen the street outside my house. The people who used to stand around in the dark – drunk and swearing – have reduced a lot. Many broken families have got together. Yes, many people have experienced change.'[7]

A year later there were still stories of God's work. In July 2007, there were reports of God's moving in three areas in Ribhoi district – Umsow-khwan, Nongrah and Lumthehsei. Meetings were conducted every day. Interestingly, this time around it was not just the children who were experiencing revival, but adults as well. The revival anniversary at Nongrah was 17 July, and the people experienced a fresh wave of the Spirit. Almost the entire congregation was moved by the Spirit, many were weeping and repenting, others were getting right with God, yet more fell in the Spirit and many were healed.

In the rural church of Nongrah, a group of women had organised a week of meetings. Nongrah is a small rural church past Smit in the East Khasi Hills. On the last day, 22 July 2007, 300 people were present for the meeting. Everyone present – from the youngest at three years old to the oldest person experienced the power of God. People repented of sins, many fell down in the Spirit, others wept over their past, and many were healed.

Pastor Barry Manuel of the Morphett Vale Baptist church from Australia ministered at the Laban church, Shillong. He taught about the gifts of the Spirit and healing in eight separate meetings. On Sunday 2 July, over forty people went forward for healing, and over a dozen testified to being healed immediately. Sheila Cherian, who connected them to the Laban Church, was there. She said 'One man in his late 60s, fell over right near my feet. His face was covered with glory dust.'

One church leader, Bah Khlainbor, under direction from the Spirit called for fasting from the people. Meeting at Pinebrook school in Shillong, 600 people pressed in to know God closely. Several had come from nearby rural areas. Many cases of demonic deliverances were seen.

Rev Lyndan Syiem from Sohra reported an unusual anniversary of the year's revival at the Nongsawlia church from 4 to 11 June. On the third night, five of the teenage girls of the Nongsawlia church, who had also been touched the year before, felt that they should prepare the church for the week-long celebration – for Jesus would be the Chief Guest. From 4 to 11 June it was like revival breaking out all over again. There were tears of conviction, deliverances, many falling under the power of the Spirit and visions amidst fervent prayer and praise.

The people of Shillong have not forgotten the Welsh Christians who first 'brought revival'. In 2007, the Presbyterian Synod met and decided to regularly pray for revival to break out in Wales, like it has in Shillong. 'There is a sense of debt that Shillong owes to the Welsh who brought the revival fire to the Khasi and Jaintia hills.'[8]

**Notes**
1. www.byfaith.co.uk/paulbyfaithtvmathewthoughts19.htm
2. Ibid.
3. Ibid.
4. Ibid.
5. Ibid.
6. http://revivalfire.info/?p=154
7. www.byfaith.co.uk, op. cit.
8. Much of this report of the Shillong Revival is from the website: www.shillongrevival.com

1. Are you conscious of the Spirit of God being within you? How do you know?

2. Why do you think a prophet is without honour in his own town?

3. How would you feel if your own home town tried to kill you?

**4**. Is your church good news for the community? How might you be part of the answer?

**5**. Despite hearing God's Word through Jesus, many fail to recognise Him. What lessons can we learn for own evangelistic witness?

**6**. The Indian believers were keen to give thanks for those who had brought the gospel to them. Are there people who shared the gospel with you for whom you are especially thankful?

# Turning the World Upside Down

**By Mike Riches**

## Author Profile

Mike Riches has served as a local church pastor (one of the churches for 24 years), ministered internationally, authored several books, and graduated with a couple of post-graduate degrees. He has a passion for the Church to be unleashed in God's emphasised presence and power to accomplish her role as God's redemptive agent in this world.

His wife Cindy has partnered with him every mile of their journey since 1974, contributing significantly in their work with her gifts and experience. Mike loves diverse cultures, travel, reading, sports and the outdoors.

# Introduction

I am fascinated by revivals in biblical and Church history. I am fascinated by the Early Church. Her birth and early development speak volumes. I love the book of Acts. It inspires and instructs. It challenges and captures me. It provides models of life and ministry that transcend time and culture. If I would summarise the Early Church I would use the phrase *simplicity with power*.

The Early Church was unsophisticated yet it defied definition. It was counter-cultural. It was supernatural – in power and life. It was irrepressible. It was characterised as *turning the world upside down* (Acts 17:6).

God's work in the Early Church is still a source of insight and instruction for revival and spiritual awakening in and through the Church. I was honoured and humbled when CWR asked if I would provide a few notes from Acts chapter 2 for their book *God Unannounced*.

I am no expert. I have experienced a measure of God's revival faith in ministry. I have experienced God's works with some similarities to the book of Acts (and the Gospels). But I know I have yet to experience God's fullest measure. We must recover God's simplicity with power in the Church for today. We are God's only redemptive option for this world.

# Preparation

**BIBLE READING**
Acts 2:1–4

**FOCUS VERSE**
'Do not leave Jerusalem, but wait for the gift my Father promised ...' (v.4)

According to Geoff Waugh, editor of *Renewal Journal*, following the trauma of World War II, spiritual life was dark and at a low ebb in the Scottish Hebrides Islands. In 1949, on the island of Lewis, the largest of the Hebrides Islands, two sisters in their eighties became burdened for a spiritual awakening and revival in their land. They devoted themselves to prayer and 'waiting on God'.

Early one winter's morning as the sisters were praying, God gave them an unshakeable conviction that revival was near. The sisters called the minister and explained their vision: 'Give yourself to prayer; give yourself to waiting upon God.'

Similarly, at Jesus' ascension He told His disciples not to engage immediately in the mission for which He had trained them. Instead they were to return to Jerusalem and wait for the Holy Spirit so as to be clothed with God's power. Only then could God's work be done.

Early in Israel's history God through Moses told Israel to prepare and purify themselves for His visit (Exod. 19:10). Later, God through Joshua told Israel to again prepare and purify themselves as He was going to do great wonders in leading them into the land He promised them (Josh. 3). They did and He did!

Let's return to the Hebrides. For months, the pastor, the sisters and the church prayed. One night at a group meeting in a barn a young deacon stood up and read Psalm 24:3–4: 'Who shall ascend into the hill of the Lord? or who shall stand in his holy place? He that hath clean hands, and a pure heart ...'(AV). He then lifted his hands and prayed, 'O God, are my hands clean? Is my heart pure?'

One account reads: 'Something happened in the barn at that moment. There was a power loosed that shook the heavens.' The rest of the story is REVIVAL SWEPT THROUGH THE ISLAND.

Charles Finney is famously known for his lecture 'Breaking up the Fallow Ground', taken from Hosea 10:12. 'Fallow ground' is an old English word used of cultivated land that is left idle. Breaking up fallow ground destroys weeds and conserves soil moisture to receive seed and rain. A fundamental principle of God in 'revival faith' is His people preparing themselves for His emphasised presence, His righteousness, His power, His revival work. Humility, purification, confession, repentance and prayer, demonstrating spiritual hunger and desperation is necessary in spiritual preparation.

**PRAYER**
**Dear Heavenly Father, may we Your people, Your Church, be overcome with hunger for Your emphasised presence. Give us Your revelation as to our need for spiritual preparation. Fill us with a new level of hunger and thirst for You and Your righteousness!**

# Expect the Unexpected

**BIBLE READING**
Acts 2:4–13

**FOCUS VERSES**
'... we hear them declaring the wonders of God in our own tongues! ... What does this mean?' (vv.11–12)

Arthur Wallis observes revival to be 'A Divine intervention where God reveals Himself to mankind in awesome holiness and irresistible power ... It is the Lord working extraordinary power on saint and sinner.'

Roy Hession in describing revival says it is '... a new entering into the fullness of the Holy Spirit and of His power to do His own work through His people ...' Jesus told His disciples to stay in Jerusalem until they received power when the Holy Spirit came upon them.

As God's emphasised presence is released so will His power be released. When His power is released you can 'expect the unexpected'. Who can contain and prescribe the power of an infinitely powerful God? Who knows best how God's power should be released in and on His people to accomplish what needs to be accomplished in them so they can be most useful for Him?

In Acts 2 God's power was demonstrated in common folks from Galilee speaking of the wonderful works of God in unlearned languages (vv.4–8). Observers were bewildered, amazed, perplexed and ridiculing. But they could not deny that something extraordinary and supernatural was at work.

God's purpose in the unexpected and naturally unexplainable is to point people to Him and His ways. It is typical in revivals for God to demonstrate Himself in supernaturally unconventional ways. In answer to the observers' questions of amazement and perplexity Peter pointed them to God, His works and His Son Jesus Christ. That is the purpose of God demonstrating supernatural works of power in times of revival.

Revival faith includes expecting God to do the unexpected. These supernatural demonstrations are God's lines of demarcation. They are designed to humble humans, to help humans see their need of and accountability to God, to restore God to His rightful place in human hearts.

As a result of Jesus' disciples' supernatural ability to speak languages in Acts 2, some asked heart-felt questions of interest (vv.7–9). Others ridiculed and mocked (v.13). The true condition of peoples' hearts was made evident. John Wimber is attributed with the saying, 'God offends the mind to reveal the heart'.

Jesus was always doing the unexpected which offended the self-righteous and self-determined. Revival faith will expect the unexpected, test it by Scripture and humble itself in submission and obedience to God. Revival faith is not limited by convention and comfort.

**PRAYER**
Lord, forgive me for my idolatry of 'control' and my prescribing limit to what You can do and how. You are all wise, all loving, and powerful. You are the one and only Sovereign, Creator God. You know what needs to be done and how. I humble myself before You and I ask You to move freely and powerfully in and through Your people. Release Your emphasised presence!

# Conviction and Repentance

## BIBLE READING
Acts 2:36–41

## FOCUS VERSE
'When the people heard this, they were cut to the heart, and said to Peter and the other apostles, "Brothers, what shall we do?"' (v.37)

Geoff Waugh writes in *Revival Fires* that Jonathan Edwards, American pastor, theologian and prominent leader of the First Great Awakening of the 1700s, published the journal of David Brainerd, a missionary to the American Indians in the 1740s. Brainerd tells of revival breaking out among Indians in October 1745 when the power of God seemed to come like a rushing mighty wind: The Indians were overwhelmed by God. Idolatry was abandoned, marriages repaired, drunkenness practically disappeared, honesty and repayments of debts prevailed. Money once wasted on excessive drinking was used for family and communal needs. Their communities were filled with love.

Common characteristics of revivals in the Scriptures demonstrate 1) a return to the true worship of God, 2) a separation from sin, 3) a repentance to obeying God and His ways, 4) a destruction of idols (that which captures the affection and trust of the people instead of God), and 5) an outbreak of love and joy.

At the first spiritual awakening of the Church, in the midst of Peter's sermon, the people were pierced to their hearts and they asked what they should do. Peter replied that they were to repent of their sins, turn to God, and be baptised in Jesus' name.

True God-empowered revivals have a distinct characteristic of conviction and repentance of sin. This must begin in but not be limited to believing followers of Jesus Christ. It will then spread to those who are not yet true disciples of Jesus.

It is through such conviction and repentance that the life of God is manifested and increased in people and communities. It does not lead to morbid introspection but instead to a true abundant life, fullness of joy and the experience and expression of God's love.

Evan Roberts of the Welsh Revival (1904) insisted that in true revival people must 1) put away any unconfessed sin, 2) put away any doubtful habit, 3) promptly obey the Holy Spirit, and 4) confess Christ publicly.

According to Oswald Smith an outcome of the Welsh Revival included infidels, drunkards, thieves and gamblers saved; and thousands reclaimed to respectability. Confessions of awful sins were heard on every side. Old debts were paid. The theatre had to leave for want of patronage. Mules in coal mines refused to work, being unused to the new kindness and good language of the miners!

Revival faith expects Holy Spirit conviction and the refreshing of repentance. That is where abundant life is experienced, people and communities transformed.

### PRAYER

**Oh Lord, forgive me for my volitional sin, for my secrets, for my self-will and my failure regarding repentance. Forgive me for quenching the life-giving conviction of the Holy Spirit related to my sin. Forgive me for redefining sin to fit my standards and desires. I need to be overwhelmed with the weightiness of Your glory and light of Your righteousness. I need to be humbled and to be ruthless towards sin in my life!**

# The More Sure Foundation

**BIBLE READING**
Acts 2:16–21,25–28,34–35,40

**FOCUS VERSE**
'And everyone who calls on the name of the Lord will be saved.' (v.21)

Throughout Church history true revivals and spiritual awakenings were ignited and sustained by the unapologetic preaching of the Scriptures. The leaders of the First Great Awakening denounced mere 'rationalist' preaching that taught mere morality.

George Whitefield and the Wesley brothers stressed the foundational doctrines of the gospel and being right with God. Jonathan Edwards reported that his sermon on Deuteronomy 32:35, 'Sinners in the Hands of an Angry God' (emphasising the truth of Romans 3:19 that humans stand before God in judgment without answer), was most effective and used by God in the 1734–35 harvest of souls in Northampton, Massachusetts.

This is no less true for Peter at the Church's first Pentecost. Peter very quickly points to Jesus. All true revivals do! He brings the Old Testament prophet Joel to weigh in on the Holy Spirit's activities on that Pentecost Day. The scriptures written by King David are then expounded on. He not only explains them but most powerfully makes the truths piercingly relevant to his listeners. He exposes their errant way of life.

True revival preaching and teaching goes beyond mere intellectual consideration. It directly challenges the inner depths of a person and personal responsibility to the truth. Peter told the Jewish audience that '*you* nailed him to a cross and killed him' in verse 23 (NLT). In verse 36 he tells them '... this Jesus, whom *you* crucified'. The result of such preaching is found in verse 37 where it states, 'Peter's words *pierced their hearts*, and they said to him and the other apostles, "*Brothers, what should we do?*"' (NLT). Verse 40 characterises true revival preaching when it says, 'Peter continued preaching for a long time, *strongly urging* all his listeners, "*Save yourselves* from this crooked generation"' (NLT, my italics). There is urgency in the message.

Jonathan Edwards' sermon 'Sinners in the Hands of an Angry God', ends with one final appeal: 'Therefore let everyone that is out of Christ, now awake and fly from the wrath to come.' Its urgency and appeal is similar to that of Peter's Pentecost message. Historical accounts of the congregation's response depict that before Edwards could finish, people were crying out, 'What shall I do to be saved?' Every true revival is characterised by a mighty demonstration of Holy Spirit power. And true revival faith rises out of allowing the truth of the Scriptures to relevantly and poignantly pierce human hearts, beginning with ours.

**PRAYER**
**Dear Heavenly Father, thank You for Your Truth embodied in Your Son Jesus Christ. Forgive me for reducing the Bible to intellectual consideration and not giving due diligence and obedience to Your Scriptures. Forgive me for not personalising and applying Your truths to my life. Forgive me for interpreting Your Scriptures to accommodate me in my lifestyle and culture instead of taking it at face value to simply obey.**

# Redefining Normal

**BIBLE READING**
Acts 2:41–47

**FOCUS VERSE**
'Everyone was filled with awe, and many wonders and miraculous signs were done by the apostles.' (v.43)

The effects of true revivals do not have a short shelf-life or pull date. True revivals help redefine normal, especially in the Church but also in society. In their book *Firefall: How God has Shaped History through Revivals*, Malcolm McDow and Alvin Reid observe that spiritual and moral declines in the Church and secular society typically precede revivals.

In such declines in secular society humans view themselves as the ultimate authority for living. God is relegated to an archaic past, no longer relevant. In such humanism society deteriorates as humans follow the inclinations of their natural hearts, which contrast with God's mind.

Similarly, the Church is swept along in worldliness and humanism. The Church becomes spiritually impotent in its adaptation to the world. It needs an invasion from God to be awakened to His glory, His truth, His ways, and His life. Then the Church is enabled to refocus its direction, redefine its mission, and reclaim its purpose for existence.

This is exactly what happened to the converted of Israel at Pentecost according to Acts 2 and beyond. Normal was redefined. Regard for Jesus was changed. Many were saved. Lives were dramatically changed into Jesus' demands for discipleship. Community was redefined in kingdom terms. They lived lives of faith, and experienced God's supernatural power and works. This redefined normal continues on chapter after chapter in the book of Acts and decade after decade in Church history.

The rewards of revival are evidenced in the lives of renewed Christians, rejuvenated churches, evangelistic results and altered moral standards. Also, when the Church is awakened, the community becomes a beneficiary of the new spiritual vitality. As revival conforms the minds and lives of believers to God's purposes, society feels the impact of such obedience.

The Early Church did not experience another Pentecost like that original day in the Church's life. But it continued to live in Pentecost's power and life. Thousands upon thousands continued to come to faith, lives were dramatically changed and communities were powerfully impacted by God's kingdom on earth. The testimony of the secular world was that the Church was turning the world upside down (Acts 17:6).

Many discount revivals as having a short shelf-life or pull date. Revival faith understands that a true revival's impact is seen as redefining normal to God's intended life for His people. And this will continue on with those who have experienced true revival.

**PRAYER**
**Oh Lord, I do look forward to my life being renewed, revived and reformed by Your life. I release my grip on what life is to look like. I am ready that the normal for my life be redefined by Your life, Your truth, Your Spirit. Release Your life and Spirit through me in power to bless others.**

# Washington State, USA – When God Invades His Church

It started following Sunday morning service on 30 January 2000 at a suburban church in Tacoma, Washington, a city 32 miles southwest of Seattle. The service had concluded and some went forward for prayer as was the custom. During the prayer ministry a young man who had gone forward began to shake and shout angrily. It became evident that he was experiencing a demonic manifestation.[1]

Pastor Mike Riches would later recall that such an event was very strange to the church and at that time they didn't know what to do about it. Up until the start of 2000, Riches would have described the church as a growing, non-denominational, evangelical church. It had established a reputation locally for its fast growing attendance, with significant growth over the previous seven years from 170 to 1,500 plus. He had pastored the church since 1983 and overseen the changes that had led to the numerical growth. He was an expository (verse by verse) Bible teacher who gave significant service time to the explanation and application of God's Word. The church had a noted children's ministry, and a vibrant young adult church, which was growing and gaining the attention of the local community. A building programme was underway to ease the space problems caused by the growth.

In many respects it was a healthy vibrant church. But God had already been at work in the pastor. He was wondering whether God had more for him personally and with the church, describing a 'holy discontent' even despite the good things that had been happening. In June 1999 he had the first indication that God would be taking the church in a new direction. He recalls: 'I was reading the verses in 1 Corinthians 4 where it says the kingdom of God is not words but power. That passage struck me as if for the first time and I heard God say, "You have given yourself to Me through My word, now will you give yourself to Me through My power?"'

It was only six months later that Mike appreciated the significance of these words from God. Starting with this demonic manifestation in late January 2000, God began to move in dramatic ways, especially in the next four months. There were prophetic words given, people were freed from demonic forces and documented physical healings occurred. A former staff member received a miraculous recovery from a debilitating condition; cancers and tumours disappeared for others. The church was asked to minister to a woman on life support, in a coma. A week later she phoned up to register her thanks. She was totally healed with no sign of the leukaemia that had brought her to the brink of death.

Mike's wife Cindy experienced an angelic visitation to explain what was happening and where it would lead. She, like him, had never been involved in the 'charismatic' movement and, like those around her, had to learn quickly how to respond to this unexpected outpouring of the Holy Spirit.

'We were on a fast learning curve,' Mike recalls. 'We began to learn a lot of truths about what I now refer to as the "two realms, one world" view. As well as the physical there is a spirit realm to the world we live in. We recognised pretty quickly that we weren't very effective at handling that spirit realm, and so began to learn truths such as the authority believers have in Christ, and how we can dismantle the foothold Satan has in people's lives. We were not equipped to cope with those first demonic manifestations. God was gracious and shut those down, but we had to get ourselves ready for everything that was starting to happen.'

The dramatic events within the church left Mike Riches and the leadership team returning to the Bible to consider the implications of what was going on.

'We wanted to help people understand what was happening so we made sure that the door was open to anyone with concerns,' he says. 'We spent a lot of time allowing people to vent their feelings one on one, or in small groups. For us it meant looking again at Scripture and discerning how we should deal with these prophetic manifestations in a practical, biblical way and then shepherding others through that.'

Mike Riches wrote a web article, 'When God Invades His Church' about the dramatic upheaval. He recalls:

> When I was in a particular state of offense at what
> God was doing in our church, He asked me a series of
> questions. 'What is My design for the Church?' 'Are you
> faithful to the commission I gave My Church, or had
> you succumbed to conventional expectations of man?'
> I then heard the Lord say, 'What is different about what
> I am doing in your church than what happened while I

ministered on earth?' 'Were there not physical healings?'
'Did I not hear directly from My Father as to what He
was going to do and what He wanted Me to do and say?'
'Were there not demonic manifestations no matter where
I ministered, whether in the Synagogue or out in the
streets and fields?' 'And did I not demonstrate authority
over all powers of darkness and powerfully release those
who had been captives?' 'Was not all of this part of
people coming into My kingdom?' 'Was not all of this
part of Me training and teaching My disciples how to
do My ministry?' 'Were not My disciples commissioned
to carry out the very ministry My Father sent Me into
the world to perform?' 'Did I not say that My disciples
would do the very works I have done and even greater?'
'Did I not pray for My disciples regarding this work and
not only them but for all who would ever believe in Me
because of their testimony?'

But many were not happy about the direction the church
was heading, and despite the open discussions and Bible
teaching explaining the way they believed God was leading
them as a church, around 70% of those who were part of the
fellowship in 2000 went on to leave. What was ironic was that
a loved member of staff was healed from a life-threatening
condition: people were pleased for him but still left the
church as they didn't have a place for that kind of activity.

Of course people took their money with them and the
planned building programme ground to a halt. Despite the fact
people were leaving, the leadership stood firm about where
they felt God was calling the church in this time of transition.

'That time of change did not mean we shrivelled up as
a church,' says Riches. 'On the contrary, many new people

were coming along as they found the power and presence of God working in the church. Also, some who did leave eventually returned when they saw that the direction we had taken was healthy.'

The wider community were also troubled by what was happening. Clover Creek Bible Fellowship had been respected in the local community as a solid and progressive evangelical church; but with stories circulating, their reputation was becoming tarnished because of the unconventional ministry that was taking place.

'The community was very aware of what was happening. Some church leaders obviously thought we had lost our moorings in the Word of God. Very hurtful things were said, especially since commitment to scripture is a pillar of our church. I'll never forget the emails that contained hurtful criticism. I struggled with that, as this criticism was sometimes coming from people I had worked alongside with mutual respect at one time.'

As much as the Clover Creek leadership sought to address the concerns of those within and outside the church, Riches maintains that significant change will always mean making decisions that will offend some.

But despite the losses of members and external criticism the church leadership remained convinced that God was at work in changing them to become a vibrant community better equipped to reach the neighbourhood with the love of Jesus.

## Postscript

Mike Riches stepped down as Senior Pastor in December 2006 to head up The Sycamore Commission, which exists to train churches and equip believers in the works and ministry of Jesus. He spent three years based in the UK working with churches that were keen to see the sort of changes in their congregations that had taken place in Seattle. He is now Senior Pastor of Harborview Fellowship Church in Gig Harbor, Washington, 45 miles southwest of Seattle, and continues to have a wider ministry which includes the UK and Europe.

**For more information on the Sycamore Commission log on to www.sycamorecommission.org**

---

### Notes

1. The basic information for *When God Invades His Church* was taken from my interview with Mike Riches on *The Leadership File* on Premier Christian Radio and an article by Justin Brierley published in *Christianity* magazine in April 2009.

1. How do you understand the phrase 'waiting on God'? Can you think of an example from your own life, or others', where God eventually came through in some way?

2. 'God offends the mind to reveal the heart?' How do you truly feel about the phenomenon associated with revival? How can you be open to God doing unusual things without being gullible?

3. Look again at Evan Roberts' advice: 1) put away any unconfessed sin, 2) put away any doubtful habit, 3) promptly obey the Holy Spirit, and 4) confess Christ publicly. What stops us doing these things?

**4**. Revival preaching focuses on Jesus. What aspects of His life and ministry would you want to stress to people you know?

**5**. What is normal, for your church? Are you happy with 'normal'?

**6**. If there was a demonic manifestation in someone you knew, what would you do?

**7**. Many people left the church that was seeing God move in power. Does this surprise you?

# Resources

In addition to the books featured already in this book:

*Great Revivalists*, John Peters (CWR, 2008)

*Why Revival Waits*, Selwyn Hughes (CWR, 2005)

*Understanding and Praying for Revival* DVD Resource Pack
(CWR, 2008)

*A Radical Encounter With God*, Greg Haslam
(New Wine Press, 2008)

The work of George Otis Jr. is featured at www.glowtorch.org
There are videos and DVDs featuring revivals, including *Let the Sea Resound*, an account of God's work in Fiji.

You can check our books by other contributors to *God Unannounced* on the web. Some are out of print but may be found second-hand.

Courses and seminars

Publishing and new media

Conference facilities

# Transforming lives

CWR's vision is to enable people to experience personal transformation through applying God's Word to their lives and relationships.

Our Bible-based training and resources help people around the world to:
• Grow in their walk with God
• Understand and apply Scripture to their lives
• Resource themselves and their church
• Develop pastoral care and counselling skills
• Train for leadership
• Strengthen relationships, marriage and family life and much more.

Our insightful writers provide daily Bible-reading notes and other resources for all ages, and our experienced course designers and presenters have gained an international reputation for excellence and effectiveness.

CWR's Training and Conference Centre in Surrey, England, provides excellent facilities in an idyllic setting – ideal for both learning and spiritual refreshment.

 **Applying God's Word**
*to everyday life and relationships*

CWR, Waverley Abbey House,
Waverley Lane, Farnham,
Surrey GU9 8EP, UK

Telephone: +44 (0)1252 784700
Email: info@cwr.org.uk
Website: www.cwr.org.uk

Registered Charity No 294387
Company Registration No 1990308

# Many people think the Bible is boring
But CWR daily devotionals are changing that!

Our range of daily Bible-reading notes has something for everyone – and to engage with even the most demanding members of the family!

Whether you want themed devotional writing, life-application notes, a deeper Bible study or meditations tailored to women or the growing minds of children and young people, we have just the one for you.

For current prices or to order, visit **www.cwr.org.uk/store** or a Christian bookshop.

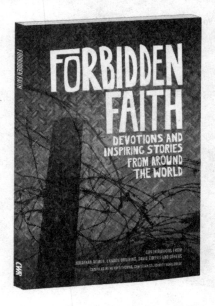

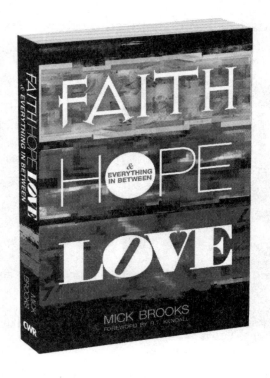

## Life is a journey, not a destination!

Although we don't all travel along the journey of discipleship
at the same rate, Mick Brooks will help you to understand that
there is a divine pattern in place and a divine pacesetter walking
with you. Themes explored include our world-view, mystery,
relationships, holiness, devotional life and much more.

**Faith, Hope, Love and Everything in Between**
by Mick Brooks
156-page paperback, 230x172mm
ISBN: 978-1-85345-598-8

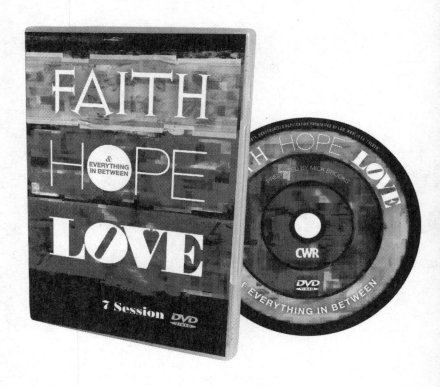

This new seven-session DVD resource for personal or small-group use provides an honest explanation of the obstacles, opportunities and questions everyone encounters in their journey of discipleship.

**Faith, Hope, Love and Everything in Between DVD**
presented by Mick Brooks
EAN: 5027957001329

For current prices or to order, visit **www.cwr.org.uk/store** or a Christian bookshop.